||| | || |||||||||| |||| | |||||||| |||
IØ161177

Just START You've Got Girl Power because of Gods Power

Stop Talking and Roll Tenaciously

Edited by Shaundale Rhodes

Manufactured in the Unites States

ISBN: 978-0-578-21812-0

*THIS BOOK IS DEDICATED TO:*

<u>Honors:</u>

*"**Mommy,** you are more than just a "Memory." She is and will always be my Mother. While her body is no longer present on this earth, she yet still lives... She lives through her children and grandchildren.*

*How do you honor a woman who gave so much of herself to others and received very little back? I do so by living to my fullest gifts, walking in my truth, understanding my power is gifted by GOD and taking nothing for granted. I do it being grateful for all the blessings and lessons. I do it knowing the chains are broken by living and walking unapologetically into my calling. Upon her shoulders I stand with Love, I walk with the dignity by which she lived and exemplified during her time on this earth.*

*Everyone says their mother is the best. I say my mine is that, best. Her levels are incomparable. My mother was perfection and purity of heart. She wasn't a saint though she was an Angel to many. I honor the one who told me I could do anything, even though I didn't always believe her... the one who loved me no matter how troublesome and stubborn I may have been. I honor the one who supported me when I became a teenage mother; I honor the one who saw and made sure I wanted for nothing; I honor the one who raised me to be my own person and to step into my gifts; and, I honor the one who always told me the truth, no matter what, and gave correction with love. I honor the one who gave me life and was there for all my "firsts". She was my biggest fan and strongest supporter. I honor the one who cried with me and for me, the one who prayed for me. We didn't always agree, and sometimes "I thought" she didn't understand me. She was truly the wind beneath my wings. And now she has real wings hovering above us all. The time has come to make good on all her sacrifices paid for. Mommy "We" Made it!! Forever Loving You!!!*

~~~~~~~~~~~~~~~~

*My Son, you did not ask to come into this world to a Mother so young and immature. You had to bear the scars and ignorance of a young girl so unaware of what it meant to be a woman, let alone a mother. I want you to know there was not one time I ever had a regret about you being born. I only wish the circumstances of my life would have been better to bring you up. If I could do it all again, I would have been more in tune with my actions and how they would affect your growth. I would show you more love, and tune your focus to not only discover, but also to believe in your gifts. I would have pushed you to create your vision.*

*I wish I could have been the mother who gave voice to what you needed to be the most successful man you could become. I am sorry that I had no voice to give you. Forgive me for any harm I caused you. Thank you for being my gift. I love you.*

*I love you more than you know. GOD gave you the best parts of me. Despite our challenges in growing up with each other, you have grown into your own. You are and will overcome all your challenges and road blocks. I am so proud that you are pushing though, turning your pain into a reward of power. I am so glad that no longer are you allowing what is designed break you take hold. Continue to channel success through resilience and strength. You are supremely gifted with the power of the written word and speech; it is to the level that it is meant to be shared with the world. Always walk in self-love and self-mastery. We never cease to learn and grow. I am so very proud of you. I'm not just talking the talk, I am walking the walk. I love you more than there are words in any language. Thank you for allowing me to be your mother.*

*To My Ladies:*

*There are some strong women in my life who deserve my unconditional love, respect and thank you. Though thank you seems rather lame. I dedicate this to my sisters and my sister-friends who have walked with me on my journey to discovery. Each one of you has played an important role in my life. You are all beautiful, strong, vibrant, and dynamic women in my life. I love you all in your own way.*

***To my Baby Sister:*** *Words don't fully express just how important you are to me. Growing up we could not have been more different—you got on my nerves like nobody's business. We weren't as close then, but there was never a break in the sister bond, no matter what it looked like to the outside world. I have always admired and envied your spunk along with your ability to captivate and enchant absolutely everyone around you. Even my friends loved you sometimes more than they loved me, I think. LOL. It's ok though, I am over it now because I realize and appreciate that you are a beautiful spirit that people gravitate to. There have been difficulties in your life, and you have always managed to see it through with grace. You are really an extension of Mommy, her Mini me. I see that too. You took on her best qualities. I pray you find that which your power, use your gifts and rise to be the beacon of light you were created to be. I love you mucho mas!!*

***To My Big Sissy:*** *They say what is understood doesn't need to be said. I think sometimes it does. We all need reminders every now and again. Blood could not have made us closer. You have always been there for me. I cannot imagine my life without you. God makes no mistakes, you were born to complete my family. I couldn't always take your tough, big sister behavior and, sometimes we would go without speaking, but I know it was all from Love and concern for me. You just don't know how much I admire you. Like the words I am saying just don't cut it. I have watched you blossom from a little girl who faced some extremely difficult realties, no little girl should have to endure and yet here you stand the woman who is about to take over the world with your Transform By Simply Doing movement. Your legacy was built through the fire you had to walk through. I am super proud of you. You are an inspiration. I love you dearly. We are about to take over the world Sissy.*

***My Nieces:*** *Babygirls, Jadahe, Elisha, Naysira, Janice, Eva, Jada, Jamela, Kayla, Melia, & Sakea; My God Daughters Quanajah and Emani, I love all of you more than you know. I want you all to trust yourselves and* decisions. You are to stand in your power. Our linage is strong. Continue to believe you can be and do anything you set out to do. Use your voice and above all Love yourselves enough to know when something doesn't feel right, it usually isn't right. Own your bodies and your mind. Don't let ANY human being tell you your value. You have Power.

**To my Nephews**: Jayquel, Farqu, EJ, Blake, Morgan Josef, &, Keith, though this book is about being a girl and a woman, never for a second think I don't love or value who you are. You are shaping up to be great men. I am so proud of you. Use your talents wisely and always walk with your head high. Live like you know you are in control of your destiny.

**To those Chicks**: My lifers **Jesscya Banks, Jenelle"Gigi"Torres, Shannon Spviey-Mayo**, and My Bestie **Chonda Ridley**, My BFF'S in this that go way back to the sand box and high school with me... I Truly LOVE YOU!!! God could not have done any better in gifting me with such longevity in my friendships. We all got stories we share. There really are just no words. So, I will sing a song from the theme of Golden Girls because I hope we get to see our golden years together, just as spunky and funny as we are now. Want to hear it? Here we go... "AND if you threw a party and invited everyone you knew... You would see the biggest gift would be from me, and the card attached would say, "Thank you for being a friend." In truth, you are more than friends; you are family.

**To my work sisters and my Usual Suspects family of sisters:** Meeting you ladies gave color to my life and brought me out of my comfort zone. You are all wonderful examples of strong vibrant women. GOD truly gave me some awesome women in my adult years. You are truly the expectation of what women should aspire to be. You are powerful, professional, fun-loving, super-intelligent, no nonsense, yet soft and beautiful women. You all have your challenges, yet you are the face of grace under fire, and I am grateful to know you all. Love you ladies.

**Spiritual Mothers Betty Fulcher, Cynthia Porter, Jacqueline McQueen and Mentors:** It is because of you that I am believing that I am a woman of God's grace, that I am a Captivating Woman, a Girl who Rocks and a Money-mover. Your teachings and motivation have given me new life. Some of you I have had the pleasure to personally and others only virtually, still you have all been in alignment with where I believe GOD is taking me. I ask that God continues to bless your gifts and that you prosper in all endeavors.

*My Virtual Mentors Thank you.*

- *Shannon Yvette*

- *Carla R. Cannon*

- *Allyson Byrd*

- *Minister Naisha Cooper*

**Last, but not least,** *I would be remiss If I did not shout out the newest support system in my life. My Mastermind Sisters* **Anita Johnson** *(Who brought us together),* **Keya Briscoe** *(Our cheerleader),* **Tina Cleveland** *(Our Energy), &* **Stephani Lee** *(Our quiet storm). With special Shout out to* **Shaundale Rhodes** *(Our check and balance) for editing my story and the positive feedback she gave me to make this writing all it could be without taking my voice out. You all have been a tremendous source of support for me. You keep me on my task and hold me accountable to my word and the love you pour out on me is nothing short of Amazing. When one of us comes up we all are going up.*

# Table of Contents

# READY SET GO!!!

Doing this afraid…. "Courage is not the absence of   fear it is doing something in spite of it." ~Les Brown

# The Self Love Letter -Little Girl

***The Love Letter:***

*Dear Little Girl inside of me,*

*Please know that I love you. I am sorry for whatever has caused you to doubt your worth. You are a beautiful soul inside and out; I want you to never forget and know you deserve every bit of the love you have given and then some. You are smart, talented, dynamic and amazing. You have a beautiful heart. If I could have shielded you from the unnecessary pains of life, I would have. I would have protected you from anything thing that would damage your spirit. I would have blocked all the dirty looks, nasty words spoken over and about you. I would have blocked the unwanted touches you received. I wish I could have reinforced how powerful you were. You are more valuable and precious than anything in this world. I would have told you never give up, that. you can dream and play big in your life. I would have showed you that it was your birthright to grow and to seek out wonderful experiences. I would have told you that even when life challenged you that you could be victorious over whatever situation you faced.*

*To the little girl inside me who still feels awkward and insecure at times know that you are perfected in God's image. You were created in love and were born to love. You can never see you the way God sees you; your spirit; your heart. The world and people around you have more enriched lives because of you being in it. Let your little light shine bright. The woman in you, who is me, promises to be your voice, and she is learning to heal, protect and empower you.*

*I am sorry that I left you alone to live in darkness, forgetting your unhealed wounds and not telling you often enough how special you are, how talented you are, and how phenomenal you are. I am sorry I didn't tell you that you did not have to play small for others to feel empowered. I'm sorry I didn't tell you that little girls with big dreams become women with vision. Forgive me for being comfortable living in fear, not believing in us—our younger version of self. Forgive me for not telling you how precious and sacred your body was in its purest form… that you should have been able to tell who hurt you and that it was not your fault or your burden to carry that shame. Forgive me for not loving you enough.*

*Thank you for growing up despite me and my choices. Thank you for not giving up when it was much easier to do. Thank you for not changing our heart no matter what happened to us as we grew into adulthood. Thank you for fighting for your beauty. Thank you for being the beginnings that is me; we are outstanding.*

*I love you Tawayna, and I will always love you. Know that as I grow in power, you will too. God is giving us Girl Power! I will hug and kiss us every day!*

*Always,*

*Your Adult Self*

# PART I: Melodious Whispers

Music can either inspire desire or incite apathy. The lyrics are written in the key of life. There is a lyric for every life situation to relate in **one's** personal life. Why do I lead with this, you wonder? In my truth, there is music. Music is poetry in motion. Music is my meditation, my vindication and my salvation. Music with its lyrics, sometimes, gives the voice I thought I didn't have. Just like words I write on this paper, I amplify and magnify loudly what is inside. In music there is no judgment or debate. You can feel what you feel and think what you think. It is freeing you to just "be", whatever that is to you. Show me a wonderful word with a soothing melody, and I will show you its power.

I often ponder what the chain of events were that led me into my current way of living. The reason was hidden from me for a long time. It was deep self-reflection that moved me to the discovery. I was beginning to ask myself some tough questions, not sure of where it would lead. On this journey, I wondered would I be afraid of the truth and could I live with what I discovered. Would it even make a difference to know? I had so many questions. Then, I realized some things and said, "I am here now, so what is next? How do we make a change?" In asking the questions, I have awakened to identify there is a greater goal at work, though I'm not sure what that is yet.

## Tawayna Nicole/Just START

I am thankful for the mistakes, missteps, losses and hard lessons, sometimes repeated until I got it. I say thank you because had I not endured, I would not have known or have discovered what I know now.

I was forced to see me. I was forced to be accountable for my decline in spirit and my lack of self- Love. Not sure exactly where it was, but somewhere I heard, "You must first lose yourself to find yourself," and it really didn't make a whole lot of sense at first. Then, it happened. I completely lost myself and had to find me again.

There was a point where didn't know who I was, who I was supposed be, or what I was supposed to do. It finally hit my ass that my life was spiraling out of control, and I declared it a state of emergency. I was in a desperate situation to get her (Me) back. I didn't want to die a spiritual death. I wanted to live because deep down I knew I deserved better. I knew misery was not my portion in life. It was time to work on me and get back all I had lost, little by little.

**I found Girl Power because of God's Power!**

## Chapter One: About Them Stones

Sticks and stones may break my bones, but words will never hurt me." That is one of the biggest lies out there. Words can and *DO* hurt. In fact, a word can mean life or death to a person. A word said in anger can cut someone down deeply, and sometimes that word lasts longer than any broken bones. In some people, disempowering words cause damage that is irrevocable. Words can wound, kill, annihilate literally and figuratively when used deliberately to take you out and you are not prepared handle what comes. When words are used to empower, they are a witness to beauty and power. Words heal, reconcile, uplift, elevate and amalgamate. Words are meant to be soul food for the spirit. Words can change lives for the better when they are said in power.

I have heard some painfully harsh words that left scarring. On several occasions, painful words heard would rub on those old wounds reopening painful memories I thought were buried deep in my soul. I would replay the words over and over just compounding on the initial hurt. All that ever did was bring me lower. I am thankful to have found words that have healing and restorative power to counteract ones of destruction. Periodically, the old hurt tried to make a comeback in the attempt to bring me low and weaken me to do the devil's handiwork for him. Oh, how easy it is to wallow in the forced, powerlessness despair and negativity brought by harmful words. **On the other side** there have also been words of empowerment and love that have regenerated my resolve, making me feel invincible—that I mattered and, most of all, that I was worthy.

Words of power, for reasons unknown to me at the time, would diminish as fast as they came. They would almost always fizzle down at a faster rate than the disempowering words I heard from others and told myself. Words of Praise were harder to hold onto in my weakened state-of-mind. It was only later in my life journey did I uncover the core truth about why. I discovered the problem was me. The problem was I allowed negative words to influence my spirit. I allowed myself to be force-fed the unconstructive and quite devastating messages. So, instead of regurgitating the poison, I filled up on the food of negative influence.

Words are like that of the fertilized embryo, which is meant to develop into a miracle of life that cultivates love upon birth, bringing a life of beauty. Words can also liken to an ectopic pregnancy, which is a displacement of life formation causing great discomfort and pain that if not excised could cause severe harm. There was a point where I wasn't growing, nor being transformed in a positive way. I, instead, lived in a state of displacement, feeling great pain, deflated and defeated. The hardest truth to openly admit to is that no one was throwing stones harder at me than I was. How do you ever win when you beat yourself up? If the world beats you and you join the party by abusing yourself, how do you win? The short and simple answer is, you don't.

Words should never be used as disempowering tools; they were created to give life. An example of that is in the Bible. The book of Genesis (chapter one, verse three) says, "And GOD said let there be..." That was the breath of formation—a call to life—and the rest, as they say, is history. Every time you utter, "I'm not good enough; I'm not pretty enough; or, I'm not smart enough, etc." you are creating your demise. When you speak low of yourself, you are living an ectopic life. You are defeating yourself. You are selling out your gifts. You are canceling out your Creator. The Bible also mentions there is power in the tongue; you can speak life or death into something.

Though I didn't see at that time of my decline, I was uttering the death call to my situation with words I spoke. I said more negative things instead of positive. I will admit, I still struggle with this some. What can I say? I am a work in progress. I can proudly boast I'm sure not where I used to be. I am armed now with more power to fight those demons.

My logic justified my double-mindedness as simply "being realistic." The rationale I used was that I was covering all the bases by hoping for the best but preparing for the worst. In hindsight, I see I had no real hope in my heart. Essentially, I was afraid of losing. This eliminated the level of expectation that breeds potential disappointment when whatever I was seeking did not work out. This was a protective mechanism in my brain, if you will. It was my comfort and, of course, I thought it worked wonders. Yet, nothing was happening and still felt wrong.

When you are thinking with a clear head, there is not much sense in that kind of thinking; there is no great return in thinking that way. You are setting yourself up to fail. I have learned that the seed you plant, and feed is the one that lives and grows. I know it is easier said than done. Like I said earlier, I struggle with it still. I have tears in my eyes as I write this because I know what it is like to feel lost and defeated. I know what it's like to want something or someone so badly, but don't want to raise your expectations out of fear of rejection. I know what it is like to choke on your lack of faith, using the tired and over-used "if it's meant to be, it will" notion.

This is where our faith is supposed to kick in. We are supposed to be trusting in God's will for us. I don't care what anyone says, that is easier said than done. We were not born with the spirit of fear, as the Bible tells us. Some people say that in times of trial is when you should pray. Well I pray every day, and there are days when I pray harder than usual because that cast of doubt is looming. I do it when I'm just about ready to prepare for the worst. I really want to say prayers of thanksgiving and not always ones of help me.  I have got to be honest, I have been angry with God or universe. I didn't trust the words or existence. If I go by what my eyes were seeing unfold, I saw nothing remotely close to what I wanted. In my mind, my prayers were not being heard. I felt forgotten and punished unjustly.  I couldn't see that I had not yet gained all I needed to receive what I thought I should. Admittedly I was only a friend of God when I got what I wanted. This gave way to not really allowing God to do what He promised. I was small in my thinking. I had to control the flow of my life and failing ever so greatly.  I began to slowly understand that my timing was not what God and the universe considered time. I had to give all of it to God. Submitting total trust and surrender has been hard.  The Bible says, "Lean not on your own understanding," and that has always been where I have gone wrong, my need to always understand.  I lived in disobedience to the word of God.

With unfiltered vision, you will see that when you're "hoping for the best," you must intend and prepare for the best. There is no need to prepare for the worst. Don't create a Plan B; this can veer you off your true path. This is what you must live and die for. There should never be an option on what you want, only a bold non-negotiable clause in place.

God set it up for us to win. Yes, there will be an obstacle here and there; it will be used as a gauge to prove you really want what you want. We often live this double-minded life. I have learned there is a rule under the force of fear; it is your foe that will never win against power that only comes from the spirit gifted to you by God.

I never allowed myself to fully desire and go after what I wanted with fierceness because deep down, I didn't believe I could have it. As time passed, I stopped asking what I wanted for my life. It never came up for consideration after a while. I let life live me. I didn't live life. I stripped myself of my dignity and my hope, and I allowed others to give more of the same in my life. As a result of the shackles placed on my head, I have made quite a few undesired, reckless and careless choices that I am still recouping from.

Upon this earth walked one who came, transitioned and transcended this life to take away the sins of the world to, to live on high and give us the fighting chance we were promised; an abundant life. He gave us the blueprint to have it, and all we had to do was trust, follow and obey the blueprint.

"When you're hoping for the best, you actually have to intend and prepare for the best." *Tawayna Nicole*

**LESSON I learned: If you want the best that is exactly what you should expect.**

In the world in which I simply existed, I just couldn't see my way clear. I had so many disempowering messages programmed in my head that when any empowerment showed up, it got silenced. Have you ever felt like you just couldn't break free from negative thinking? If you have, please don't believe the lies. I am here to tell you that you can break free. It's not so easy yet is very possible.

I learned it boils down to answering the question, how bad do you want change? You've got to put it into terms of life and death. I don't know anyone who "wants" to die. I think for some who have committed a successful suicide they felt it was the only way to stop the hurt and I understand for countless people in moments of despair some may see death a better option, yet it really isn't. You can't undo death; however, if you can make it to the next day, then you get another chance to fight and make things better.

You must make a conscious decision to live. That means doing the hard work and pushing through the pain to jumpstart your inner defibrillator, bringing you back to a conscious state-of-mind, and letting the healing begin. I am I here to tell you ALL things are possible, even when life seems impossible. (Whoa... As I write this, even I am amazed that I just wrote that last statement because there was a time when I didn't believe even the possible was possible for me. It is a daily battle for me still, and yet I get through because I just have the coolest life reviver on the planet.)

Excuse the cliché, I'm in it to win in this life. That is why I push myself when things don't go the way I need them to, or when the things are out of my control and can knock the wind out of my sail. I get reminders as I see prosperity in life all around me. I believe I am part of that life; I just have to go after it and believe that it's mine.

## Tawayna Nicole/Just START

I'm not a preacher or a teacher; however, I am woman finding her voice. I feel sharing what I have learned is a good thing. I do this in the hope of letting another woman know she is not alone on her journey, helping her to find her path, so that she can overcome the darkness and step into the light of GOD's love and get her power to fuel her being.

In the light you will be able to see all the wonderful and empowering words you have lacked for so long. You will see yourself the way God sees you. Your spirit will begin to calibrate at a higher frequency and operate on a greater level. No, this is not an overnight process; however, if you put in the work, you will feel the difference even in moments of trial. You will begin to find your power. You will find God's love in self-love. You have no right not to love yourself because you were created in the image of The Most High, and God doesn't make junk.

Do you have the life you want? What would be utopia for you? What would your ideal life look like? The short of it for me is to live a spirit-filled, abundant life that includes marriage to the love of my life, being a successful business woman, and being wealthy in all areas, my health, finances, etc. I want to see my son be his greatest self, for my family and my other loved ones to no longer live in bondage of whatever stifles growth and movement to the next level. I want to be in flow, not conforming to the standards of the world's ideas or ideals. I want to be a blessing to someone else wherever I am capable and useful to them. I want the opportunity to frolic running free, traveling and enjoying the blessings of my life. I want everything. I repeat loudly this time, I WANT EVERYTHING GOD has for me. I want it all. It may take me some time, but I am coming for ALL that has been promised to me.

There was a time when I honestly could not conceive, let alone believe, having it all was possible for me. Do you want to know what I learned? I learned that I had to reprogram my thought process. I may stumble and fall along the way, yet I will continue to pick myself back up. I had to believe in myself enough to begin to change the dialogue in my head. I have serious conversations in this head of mine. I think so much, I think on my thoughts. Can you say "overwhelmed" to find the narrative that speaks to me, that calls me to action to be of consequence in this life?

Most of the time, I was always second-guessing everything I said or thought. Doing this had a negative impact on how things went for me. I, being so unsure most of the time, found it easier to hold a lot of things in. This led to many missed opportunities. It also allowed for some abusive actions to take place. I was not the true leader of my life as I was born to be. My personal life was out of control. The only place I felt somewhat confident with some order was in my workplace. Even that was not without its challenges, still it was my comfort zone and I could hold firm to what I knew.

I find that I don't second-guess myself nearly as much as past times. The conversations in my head push a more positive dialogue, even when the situation looks insurmountable. My step is stronger; my stature is taller. I am becoming at ease while I am walking unapologetically. The woman in me is a perfect package. What will come to define me as time progresses is that I refused to give up on attaining higher levels of being.

# Chapter Two: Now What?

I t's easy to tell people to "pray and give it to God". I

don't know how many times I had been told that and said the same to others. To some degree I think it is what people say when they don't know the answer. At the same time, it's wise and possibly, the better solution because it removes undo influences. It takes away the "if I were you" advice that you know darn-well would be a different action if they were you. There were times when I didn't always listen or take my own advice about giving it to God. I thought *why, when I can fix it myself.* Besides, I felt this God wasn't helping me anyway, remember? I questioned the validity of God's existence. It is always easy to tell someone what to do when you are not the person with the challenge. Even if you are coming from a place of experience in a similar situation, it is not your story. I stopped giving advice, and I stopped taking advice. I walked my own road of solitude.

Trying to Seek this God, I would pray, read the bible, and attended church regularly. I was an active member in various ministries at the church I was attending. Yet, it had no life for me—no real meaning. The Spirit was not there. Praying did not have a purpose, and nothing changed for me.   The Bible was just a book of words written in another language to me. The Bible was very hard to bring to life due to my inability to understand. It might as well had been written in invisible ink because I couldn't see or understand what it was saying.

 After my mother became ill, my church attendance started to dwindle ever so slightly. I would make "church visits" here and there. I would sit in the back, so I could get in and get out... just saying that I went. I wasn't growing in my spirit there. Honestly, I don't think I ever felt at home there. For reasons I can't quite pin point, I just didn't. The people were nice enough, and there were even those few I connected with outside the doors. Maybe I didn't make enough effort. Who knows? What I do know now is that it really wasn't a fit for me. I could not admit then. My mother was the last reason I attended, and now she had gone. She passed away on May 28, 2013, which happens to also be my son's birthday, and I can count on my hands how many times I have been back there since her passing.

I saw blessing after blessing in the lives of others being delivered from their afflictions. I knew miracles were real. I somehow didn't see my life set up for miracles and blessings. I say my life was just one big misunderstanding. My topsy-turvy world showcased the opposite of almost everything I coveted or thought. For the love of Christ, I could not figure out what I did so terrible that my life was turning out the way it was. It sounds so desperate—like I lived in dire straits in the gutter, by world's standards. The reality is, it wasn't that kind of desperation, but for my life it was a desperate one. It wasn't the worst life a person could live just not the best one I wanted to live. Not being able to pin point the origin of error was almost maddening. Part of me felt like my life was a failure, as a Daughter, as Mother and as a Woman.

I felt I failed as a mother because my son didn't have both his parents in his life. I didn't know enough, nor could I supply all he needed to grow whole and powerful enough to keep away the soul-hurt. How could I, living in my own hurt? I learned that my son didn't feel nurtured or loved. He felt alone most times, which manifested into a poor relationship we had that that lasted too many years.

Then there were my feelings of failure as a daughter because my mother and I didn't always see eye-to-eye on things. We had very different personalities. My mother was one of the most supportive people in my life though. I knew she loved me; there was never any doubt. There were times though she didn't always like me as a person. I'm sure most parents have gone through that stage with their children. I know I went through it with mine. I probably took it more to heart than I should have.

As a daughter, I felt like I had not lived up to what I thought were my mother's "impossible" expectations. Not so much of what I should do with my life, but more of who I should be. She would always be encouraging of my whims. She would tell me that I was all she dreamed of when she was a little girl. She told me I was perfection in her eyes and encouraged whatever I wanted or didn't want to do. I suspect she saw greatness I couldn't see. My vision was short-sighted in that I couldn't be her dream, not realizing she only wanted me to be my own.

Mommy said I could be anything I chose to be. The thing was how? How could I be anything I wanted? What example did I have? I know my mother was not living the life she really wanted. I pondered those words to ascertain what she meant by "anything" when the world around me sent a different message. The messages vibrating at a frequency that decoded I was nothing much, average at best. I didn't see EXTRAordinary in me. How when I saw my mother struggle and battle her own personal demons, the ones she tried to hide from us, but were so much a part of her being that we could see the sadness through her smiles and laughter? How could I know that what I saw in my mother was a true testament to how extraordinary I really was, and was also the woman I was born from? How could I know that?

Growing up what I saw through my visual eye as a girl, and even into my adult years, was not the truth of her. It was her current circumstances; it was her life. All I saw was how she dealt with her pain and not being able to overcome, and just accepting what it bore her. There were many times when I saw her just check out, and I saw it as weakness. What I know now was that my mother chose to live. What I know now is that she had a quiet, inner strength that would float to the surface from time-to-time. She was determined to see her children excel where she did not.

As a woman who is going through and working to overthrow my own challenges, I understand she survived her way. I understand that if she wasn't filled with something special, she would not have made it through the heavy trials she carried throughout her life. Mommy was a powerful and extraordinary presence in my life. I was to be an extension of that and take it to the next level. As the song says, "I was blind, but now I see." My mother had extraordinary love. She had an unwavering and unfailing love for everyone who touched her path, and it shone ever so brightly at her Homecoming service. I was greatness and born for it.

Then, there were those feelings of failure as a woman. My relationship track record sucked. I felt uncared for, devalued and therefore, cautious. There seemed no other common denominator, but me for these failures. Of course, I had to be the problem, right? I was not caring enough, pretty enough, devoted enough, or too much. I don't really know. I decided that the failures were due in part to just not being a right fit for me. You know, that if "it's meant to be, it will."

Thing was, I knew going into certain relationships that they were doomed from the beginning. I never felt any connection in my soul with them, though I would try to work it out. I thought that was what you were supposed to do. Knowing this, a person would wonder why I even bothered to waste my time, energy, and invest my feelings. What I told myself was that nothing was easy or perfect all the time. I lied and I told myself at some point you must compromise but it was really settling. Love can grow on you and you can work through and overcome any challenges. The relationships weren't fulfilling they didn't edify me, they drained me. When the actual relationships ended for whatever the reasons were, I felt nothing in terms of my life being over without them. I felt some sadness of course if I came to care about them however, there was no real, deep love which allowed me to move on quickly. Funny enough even though I knew none of them were the one it still felt like I failed.

I wanted a connection to have that feeling of home in someone... one who made life so much better with than without, the man who saw the beauty and beast that is me and still believed I was flawless. I wanted a man who saw the independence as a mask for protection. I wanted him to see that I really needed his covering and love. I was kind of forced to watch other women reap the love I gave the men I had been with prior. It is not a good feeling at all. I had to come to terms that my purpose in their lives was fulfilled and that it wasn't mine. They were not mine. Still it did not ease the thoughts of my failure as woman. It felt that way because I was unable to make what I knew a lie. I struggled with how I would become great when I didn't feel I was.

I couldn't see my way clear to live up to the standard Mommy, had set me up for. I'd had way too many moments of feeling inadequate, more so as a woman because I had one unfulfilled relationship after another. I snuffed out opportunities of bringing new life in this world. I terminated pregnancies because I didn't want to be another statistic in the books as a multiple-time single mother., I was already branded as a teenaged single mother. I had no husband or solid relationship. Being what now seems to be the new norm wasn't going to work for me. I had the visual of what life was supposed to be and just enough wasn't enough.

**Learning to Be a woman:**

My twenties were what I like to categorize as my growing pains decade. I was young, single and raising a boy child. I wasn't looking for a father for my son; I was seeking a man for companionship who would accept I had a child. During that time in my life, I don't know that I was ready for what I was asking for in all honesty. Truth be told I didn't have an expectation at all. A relationship was just something I thought was supposed to happen and carry you off into happily ever after. When that didn't happen the way I thought, I really wasn't bothered. In this time of my life there was no pressure for me to be married. Admittingly, part of me had hoped to have been married during that time. It just was not a big deal that I wasn't. I simply focused on maintaining gainful employment, so that my son would have everything he needed and having a good time.

It wasn't until my 30's that discomfort with having the unmarried status set in. This is supposed to be the decade where you are on a direct path to your goals (if you had any to start) had you not reached them already by now. You were supposed to be financially stable and you were beginning to settle down with a partner, at least that is what I had in my mind anyway. I had not one thing achieved. It seemed as if everyone in the world was in love, married, and financially well off except me. **Adding** insult to injury, there were men I had previous relationships with starting to get married, which felt like it was happening off my back. I had a few who had the nerve to still want the benefits of being with me during their marriages without having to be obligated to me. My energy had to be on a low frequency that they even thought that I would entertain such nonsense. Many of things I may be and many a thing I may do but the one thing I won't do is be ripped to the white meat of who I am. I refused to lose my dignity. There wasn't enough love in my heart sell myself as cheaply as they thought.

To even think of me in such a cheap manner was hurtful and influenced my closeted negative lies I believed. I wanted to be a married woman myself one day. I just could not even begin to imagine violating another woman that way. Shame on them. I saw firsthand what something like that could do to a family.

Mommy and I had a running joke that I made husbands for other women. I realize now I gave life to those thoughts. This joke really wasn't very funny at all because it was at my expense and my pain. I guess that was my gift to the world to create better men for other women. I wondered in agony if that really was my role, to be the husband-maker. If I would have known I was so successful at molding men into husbands, I would have made a business out of it and made some money. I was only mad because I wasn't making one for myself. I can truly laugh at it now. It's not funny when you are picking yourself apart to find out why it wasn't you, continually wondering what is wrong with yourself.

Question after question, I asked myself daily almost in a madding type way like: What was I doing wrong? Why wasn't I good enough to marry? I could not understand it. My close friends who knew the inner workings of my heart would do what any good friend would do if they are hurting. They would try and ease me and toughen me up by saying I deserved better, I was too good for them, too smart, they didn't deserve the love I gave, or I gave too much, blah blah blah. None of those messages could resonate. "I'm too good?" "I gave too much?" Say what? There is no such thing as "too good". What I heard was I wasn't' enough; I wasn't good in any of it because they left or allowed me to leave.

I mean, I would go through everything that I thought could possibly be wrong with me from my physical attributes to my social and mental ones. Then, I blamed God. I just knew I was being punished for something. I couldn't tell you what that "something" was, but I had to have done a terrible thing for my life to be as it was. Then, after a time I stopped figuring; I stopped blaming and accepted life as it came no matter how it came. In short, I gave up. I decided I wasn't winning, and I would accept my lot in life as is.

I wasn't at ease with my surrender to life living me. I just didn't know what to do, so I lied to myself knowing deep down I deserved better. The dissatisfaction in me was so intense, I could feel it from time-to-time—this little rumble inside me that screamed NO this IS NOT your life. This was not God's plan. I deserve better. It just wasn't loud enough of a voice to win over the negative voices at that time.

# PART II: Change in Frequency

I really cannot tell you much about the day that

caused the shift, only that this was a dark time in my life that was super-painful. I have tried to come up with an adjective for it, and there is none. The best I can come up with is my heart was ripped from my body alive with no anesthesia. In short, I died a spiritual death. I had gone through a separation, the loss of my mother, my son and I were at odds, then there was the added stress on the job. Though it didn't all happen at the same time, I didn't get to breathe in between. There was no time to fully process any of it. I felt like I was going insane. Oh, my goodness, I got to a point where I could not eat or sleep, and my mind would not shut up. The tears were like oceans. The distorted tainted voices in my head were like a broken record, or in more modern terms a video on loop. It was my worst nightmare awake in the daytime. I always felt like I was on an episode of *Punked*.

The words that were infiltrating played over and over. They were so ugly—so harsh—and coming down like a thunderous wrath of God. It was almost deafening and destructive. It was in that moment when I broke down like a used car in the middle of oncoming traffic. The pain was so prodigious, I thought for a split-second death might be better. It was a challenge to breathe; I was dizzy, faint and I just knew God was about to call me home. I was almost ready to go. The tears were unstoppable, my heart was beating so hard in my chest it hurt. It was volatile, life-shattering. I was having the big one I thought. I think I stopped breathing for a moment. I let out this noise which came with so many tears I could flood my neighborhood. It was mass destruction. I couldn't eat for days at a time and when I did, it came back up. I was taking time off from work. I was never too far from my bed, although I couldn't sleep when I laid down. I was weak as a newborn colt, as fragile as a porcelain doll. I would be in the street and just cry without provocation. I don't know how I got through the days sometimes. Some nights I would have to take over-the-counter medicine to help me sleep. I'd go to sleep crying and wake up crying. I cried a lot, sometimes at the most inconvenient times and places. I was miserable. I was essentially alive and not living. It was nothing but GOD's mercy that brought me out. No one really knew I was going through this session in my life. The tears of a clown.

For me, this was a culmination of life. I was already weighted down, and it was a feather that fell and knocked me out for a while. There had been a series of traumatic events over the years. I have always been "strong" on the outside for so long, never admitting I was dying a slow death on the inside. The pain went longer and deeper than I can even begin to tell you.

"GOD WHY??" I screamed and cried. I was so tired and angry at HIM. I kept saying I don't deserve this kind of pain; I don't deserve this unfulfilled life; and, my son should not have to suffer for my sins either. Make him whole and happy. I just wanted it to stop. I was angry, I was hurting, and I felt the world was crashing down on me, stripping the last bit of dignity I had left.

I was lost, and I didn't even know that I was. I had questions. I wanted answers. I had to ask. I wanted to know why. What did I do wrong, and what could I do to fix my wrongs? I just could not take another moment of feeling so worthless. My life in the lyrics of Dion Farris:

## Tawayna Nicole/Just START

"Goodbye Morning, sorry it had to end/but see I cried just a little too long/Now it's time for me to be strong/…. Now it's time for me to move on.    I wanted to be one of the people who told their testimonies about God's miracles in their life. It's not that I didn't have blessings in my life. I didn't feel they were because it didn't fill the vison I saw. I had to come to place of maturity to fully understand that. I had doubtfulness that surfaced because it just wasn't the way I wanted it, and I subconsciously felt undeserving.

It was a process to get to where I started to believe I did deserve for God to love and bless me fully. After all, my creator gave me life. HE created me in love. Then, one fine day with all I had left in me, I got down on my knees with a desperate prayer. I didn't do it because someone said that it is what I should do; I didn't seek council from a spiritual leader who said I should. It was of my own flow in spirit. It wasn't until I was broken that the light shone on the darkness was exposed. I begin to open to the wonderful possibilities of I can. It allowed me the desire to delve deeper and make a change.

I'm singing a new theme song by Mary Mary because it is the way I see myself…. "It's the God in me that makes me so fresh, that makes so clean, that makes me so sweet." That's why I can't stop—won't stop—getting on my knees to give it all to GOD, through the Divine Savior. Now does that mean I have fully achieved my complete shift? Not yet, but I am expecting it any day now, and then that will be another story.

# Chapter Three: With God There is Power

W hen you fully trust and believe in a higher

being than yourself, you walk differently, you act differently and, most importantly, you feel differently—and it radiates to the world. You know those the stones you are throwing at yourself, guess what? God blocked them sending them back to where they came from, the pit of darkness, and they should never be picked up to be thrown again.

Ladies, women of God, believers of something, or a universe greater than yourself, you can be transformed by your own words. I promise you that it is possible. You must fight to believe that it is, too. You are not alone in this. You get you some sisters/friends to lift you up until you can stand in your own power. They will stand in the gap until you find your footing in God/Universal being that catapults you to the level of elevation you desire.

Each one teaches one; sharing is caring; and I am here to share because I care about you. Some of you are me, and I am some of you. We are a Sisterhood. I am my sister's keeper, and she is mine. Girl Power because of God's power!!

## Tawayna Nicole/Just START

I had forgotten that I came from a lineage of strong women on both sides. I realize now that I have surrounded myself around equally strong female friends and associates. I had the power all along, I just needed to discover it for me, and you can too.

In the age of social media, people are making larger connections in more areas than ever before. I have made a few lifelong friends as a result. I have been part of many social media groups and, on one of those day days, a Women elevate each other support group had so many posts of women who were hurting in one way or another. The pain from different diasporas, for many different reasons. Can't say what it was, but I was led to say pray for them. Now, I'm not comfortable with being an intercessor because I always thought my words/prayers weren't eloquent enough to be expressed aloud. I didn't feel I was worthy to pray for another in that manner. The negative voice within me said I wasn't, but I silenced that awful voice and prayed anyway. I came from a place of love and purity; therefore, it was good enough. It touched who it was supposed to touch, and I also shared it with my close personal circle of sisters and friends. Right now, I share it with you. I don't know who needs it. If it touches you, then it was for you and any woman reading this. I have done what I was meant to do.

*Ladies, I uplift you in prayer calling on the name and blessing of Jesus Christ to comfort, heal, anoint, and prosper all who are in need. Create a right spirit and mind. Keep us in your care; help us to fight the good fight, that no weapon formed destroys our faith in Your plan for us. Thank you, Lord, for abundant lives You call us to lead. Your word said You withhold no good thing, that You will restore and make room for the new blessing. Make rivers in the desert. Make roads in the wilderness. Your daughter's need You now, Lord. Meet us where we are. Bless us according to Your will, so you get the Glory. In the name of Jesus, ease the pain of my sisters. I claim strength, abundance, prosperity, healing, health, wealth, wholeness, clear direction, a sound mind and heart in the name of Jesus. I speak life over every situation in their lives that produce no fruit. I am giving YOU the glory. Thanking YOU for your continued blessing... in the name of Jesus. Amen. I lay this prayer at the throne of grace. Thank you, Lord. Amen!*

I have come to believe in the power of prayer. It transforms; it transcends; it solves, gives clarity, elevates, and it heals. What I have achieved is a greater sense of self and empowerment to change my situation.

I come unapologetically firm in my belief in myself, knowing I have a champion within me and angels surrounding me, guiding me to my greatest self and to the desires of my heart. It took me some time to find my wonderful words, and I want to help you get to yours like did. I'm going to say throughout this book, I am not a preacher or a teacher. I aspire to inspire another woman to rewrite her story and to change her words that will change her life to walk in her own Girl Power and S.T.A.R.T!

You are meant to show up fully in your expression as a woman. Own your Woman humanness. Own who you are, own your flaws and all of what makes you glorious. Be the mistress of your life that you were born to be. You are truly in control of your life. God will open the doors you want open to you, if they are for your good. God will even open some that are not because He gives the desires of your heart. You know the saying be careful what you wish for because you just may get it, right?

We truly must change the way we think because the way we think will dictate our level of action. I have learned and am still learning how the one rephrasing of a statement can change the whole story around.

*"Because we must be before we can do, and we can only do to the extent to which we are, and who we are depends on what we think." ~Charles Haanel~*

How do you change your thinking, you may ask? You are changing it by using just one positive word at a time.

I'm not an expert on what to do to transform you. I am just a woman writing to show another woman who may be going through, she is not alone. I can only share what is happening for me and maybe inspire change in you to S.T.A.R.T using your Girl Power.

If at the end of this journey I am taking you through, you still can't find your way clear to the change, I will refer you to women who can walk you through step-by-step in achieving that change. These are women in my opinion A1 awesome. They have inspired and mentored me in some way. Some I have had up close and personal encounters, while others have done so virtually to bring me this level of power. They are women of God, women of the spirit, and intuitive souls. They are women who understand their power and are building empires. They are ministers, authors, intuitive healers, life coaches, therapists and financial wealth builders who are sharing their gifts and allowing them to pour into other women on their path to wholeness.

It is not easy, and girl it gets ugly. But, guess what? You don't have to go it alone. You have a tribe of sisters, known and unknown, to support your journey to a more powerful you. You have to do the work because no one will force or pull you to do anything you don't want to do. No one can change you, but you. I will encourage you to get on moving. Like the Trailblazer Carla R. Cannon, would say "If you always do what you always did, then you will always get what you always got." Now, say that 3 times fast.

My question is again: how bad do you want change? How bad do you want to feel free from fear and walk in power? It's work, and ladies I'm still working. The hardest thing to do is unlearn something hardwired into your brain and learn a new way when it comes to personal journeys. It is amazing how we will quickly adapt to the latest and greatest technology and forget about the old but can't do that with our own lives. I'm not where I want to be; I'm just not where I used to be, and now I can see who I'm supposed to be. There ain't no cookie-cutter easy fix. I'm a work in progress. God is not through with me yet.

*"If you always do what you always did, then you will always get what you always got".*

*Carla Cannon, The Trailblizer*

You won't go to sleep and wake up transformed the next day. There will still be days that bring you low. I ask you not to allow those days too much life. Find your center to improve your soul calibration. Like Popeye when he felt weak and low, he ate his spinach and was on full power. Call on God/ or your spirit guide to strengthen you. The works and words of the Bible give strength. I will share some passages to read that have been handed to me that gave and continue to give me power and the weapons I need. Fast, pray and believe. I am love, comfort, harmony, support, strength, courage, and elevation. I am abundance, and overflow made to perfection who so happens to be a flawless beauty. I am a Masterpiece, aged to perfection.

Our truth and power come from a source, a spirit from deep within that calibrates far above our surface. I suggest that you seek spiritual council from someone who is grounded and knowledgeable in the word. Call on God through connection to the Divine Savior. If you feel you can't go it alone, call or text message someone who can call for you until you gather your strength to do it yourself. I am learning all about intercessory prayer, and it can be your most powerful weapon. Mathew 18:20 says, "If two or three are gathered in my name, there I am with them"

I don't want to omit men completely from our growth process, as they are very much an integrated part of who we are as women. Admittedly or not, some of the things we do and who we become are predicated upon men and how they see us. Masculine council is also a part of the process. They have words of wisdom too, if you have the ears to hear and mind open enough to receive truth. You really can learn a lot from a man about who he is and more important about yourself and the role you wish to design and play out in life.

You've got to be willing to get honest and dig deep in order to clean out the dirt, to shine a light in the dark places. My mind was set up like an episode of hoarders. I still had stuff from 1975 when I was four years old up in there. It was messy. It is only then will you see what negative words are hiding and waiting for their chance to make a comeback. And you've got to be ready to fight the fires of hell to get them gone, burned and buried forever.

It's time to live in your authentic power, position and purpose... Ladies, we are at WAR!!!! Fight to re-gain and reclaim your life, enlarge your territory, harness and use the Power of God!! The battlefield of the mind is real, and you must train your mind to fight and your weapons are supplied in the word of God. *Jerimiah 50:34 "The Lord*

Tawayna Nicole/Just START

*opened his Armory and has brought out weapons of his indentation for the work..."*

Intentionally blank:  For the Breakout thoughts

# Chapter Four: Changing thoughts

*Let's change the dynamic of our thinking...*

H ere is how I did it and you can too. I wrote
myself couple of lists. One is about who thought I was,
the other was about how I viewed myself, and lastly what
I wanted for my life. I have many notebooks, journals,
doodles, sticky notes, and torn envelops—you get the
picture. If a thought comes, or I hear something I want to
remember that speaks to me I write it down.

I am always writing something down. I look back on
some of them from time to time, and I see just how far I
have come from where I was. Some of my earlier writings
had me asking what in tarnation was I thinking. Some of
it was dark in content—the woe is me syndrome. It was
self-defeating. I don't think I realized how sad of a person
I really was. Thankfully trouble doesn't last always, and
there were some light-hearted ones. My writing is the
voice I felt I did not have. Writing allows me to say what I
cannot verbalize. I always stayed away from large
conversations, fearful of being misunderstood and
revealing ignorance of any kind. I still don't know where
that fear came from. Writing allows me full expression,
though there are times when I haven't been truthful to
myself by censoring my own voice. All I can say now is
thank GOD for my growth and elevation. I have been

blessed with a lot of love, pain and beauty in my words. They were transformative components.

The assessment template I am going to share is what has helped me see some things more clearly, and you can do this whenever you are ready but, what better time to S.T.A.R.T.... than now? I guess by now you are probably wondering what the acronym S.T.A.R.T is all about, as you have seen it a few times throughout the book. Have you made the connection? You will find out soon enough if you haven't, and I hope when you do you will find it just as cool as I did.

I won't be there when you create your list. This is your private journey, about your truth. If you decide to take this journey, I want you write honestly and hold grace for yourself. I won't be able to quantify or qualify your list because, for starters, I won't see it and will be unique to you. All I will say is if your columns of improvements are more than your perfections, then you have some real soul and mind work to do. Words of strength give you power, while words of weakness pull you down in spirit. Find out what forces your weakness, and then find out what can power up your strength.
*Sample listing

| PERFECTIONS /STRENGTHS (Words of Power) | IMPROVEMENTS/WEAKNESS (Words of Force) |
|---|---|
| I am Intelligent | Shy around others |
| I am Loyal | Too standoffish |
| I am Accepting | Controlling |
| I am Considerate | Self-Destructive behaviors |
| I am Appreciative | Jealous |
| I am Attractive | Secretive |

| I am encouraging | |
|---|---|
| I am a Good person | |

Some of you may feel challenged by this listing to pull out what you like about yourself. As for the rest of you, may be a breeze. If you are anything like me, it was a bit challenging to say the least. The first time did I this list, it was hard for me writing out what I liked about myself, but could I write for days about what I didn't like about me. I was my own worst critic. Good grief.

Don't over-think it. I don't want you to spend too much time writing. It's got to come from what's fresh and most prominent in your mind. You don't want to give yourself a chance to second-guess and edit your thoughts because it won't be a true interpretation of what your inner-voice is really saying to you. I would suggest you spend no more the 15 minutes on your list and try not to put too much emphasis on your dislikes. Besides, if you have to think that hard, then you are like a little kid on a sit and spin—getting dizzy and making yourself sick. This is not a how to beat yourself up list because when you do that it makes you get weak. And let's face it, the world will beat us up enough; we don't need to help it.

**We are** about building ourselves up and receiving our power. The dislikes are a simply written visuals, of what is in the storage closet of our mind, that we are going to reorganize. The first thing we must do is take everything out and sort through it to see what we want to keep or throw away, then reorganize in a better way. If there is anything that is no longer useful (aka thoughts), we are going to purge the garbage... the lies we've been told by others and by ourselves that make us feel unworthy. We are going to take those negatives and replace them with affirmatives. We are going to replace the garbage with words that build us up and sustain us by using words that give us Power.

We don't want to, at any time, get fixated on the problem. It's not easy to do. I know, I still have bouts of "oh, I don't like this or that about myself, or I need to fix that." The only thing truly wrong with me was I had the spirit of unbelief and the wrong thoughts about myself. Once I got wind of this powerful and transformative message, I realized I'm... well... I'm just freaking awesome—flaws and all. I am working towards balance and clear perceptions.

The only thing that changes a problem is a solution. If you want to change and nothing is changing, then you might want to look at what you're doing to promote change. The definition of insanity is doing the same thing over and over and expecting a different result.

My suggestion for now would be to look at your list of P/I and focus on the things you like. Focus on your strengths. Since we already know you will have no trouble believing the negative things, it's important to reinforce the affirmatives. It's easier to berate than to praise. It's not a humble, nor is it a noble, gesture to dumb yourself down, or dim your light to make others feel better about themselves. I have often wondered why it is much more acceptable to agree with the negatives than positives about ourselves. Well ladies, it's time to change the conversation and the way we think. I believe that if you focus on the positives, the negatives will eventually fall away. It will only work if you work it.

> *"It is time to change the conversation and the way we think."* ~Tawayna Nicole

What I have come to learn is that the power of right thinking is what makes successful people thrive. What makes my life successful today is not just that I have obtained financial wealth, or that I have a super-awesome career that leaves a legacy to last the ages (although that is a part of my vision, Manifesting that right now). What makes me successful is that I have changed the view of how I see myself. I see myself bigger and better than my current situation would have me believe. I am a powerhouse because I am finally seeing that I have chosen not to give up when some would have.

I no longer walk in paralyzing fear, self-doubt and despair. In doing that I can stand a little taller, though not in height, as I am taller in the Spirit. I have grown in confidence, I am growing to become fearless, and I have grown to be unapologetic in who I am evolving into. I have been able to accept and acknowledge my complete beauty and intensify my power to build the life I envision. I have started to step out of my comfort zone. I am successful because every morning I wake there is a little bit of faith and a whole lot of love. There is will, and there is opportunity to change life for the better one moment at a time. Who I am today is the tone I set yesterday.

Mommy would say to me and my sister that we could do and be anything we wanted. The key to this is I learned is to totally believe in yourself, your abilities and your gifts. You might ask the question like I did: How do you know what your gifts are? Some of us know sooner than others, and that is ok. I will let you in on a little secret, I am still finding out what my gifts are. I know in part that whatever it may be, service of some kind is involved. We all have paths of discovery to walk and their lies the beauty. The beauty is that it's tailor-made, according to your specifications and in that your levels will never be able to be compared to anyone else, though they may try. In this walk your only true competition is you and yourself. So have fun with it. You're not restricted to one avenue, you're not on a "must have it done" due date unless you set it. Explore all of what comes to you. What I am finally understanding is that what we think about, we bring about when we act.

In all of the books I have read or, listened to, and seminars I have attended, they have all across the board reverberated the same teaching; success in life will depend on the power of your thoughts. They all teach your mindset can make or break your life, and that it is important that you get control of your mind. It is your thoughts that dictate your action or inaction. The first person who should believe in you, is you. There was a saying you are what you eat, and so it goes for the mind; you are what you think. Even the Bible confirms in Proverbs *23:7, "As a man thinketh in his heart, so is he..." When* you recognize and fully understand this... when it sits in your spirit... you will start to look more closely at what is clogging your mind.

We all have something that makes us special, a little something that makes us stand out from the pack. We all have one or two things that only belong to us. Explore them and, most of all; don't be afraid to share them. Some gifts are not as tangible as maybe writing a story or singing a song.

Some gifts are of the spirit, like how kind you are to children or someone more unfortunate that you have helped with something simple or challenging. Did you know the ability to make someone laugh is a gift? The ability to garner smiles and laughter are extremely powerful gifts. You never know you might have saved a life by something as small as a hello. There is no qualifier or quantifier on what could be considered a gift. Bringing someone from sadness to joy is a most precious gift, too. Laughter has healing powers. I vow to do more of it. So, don't discount anything you do, no matter how infinitesimally small it may seem to you.

As I am going through this journey, I have gained a confidence that I never had before. I stepped out of my comfort zone to write this book. I have started and stopped short so many times, I have lost count. I can't help but feel I have something to offer to someone out there, and I dare not be afraid to step out. I don't want to miss my blessing to be a blessing.

I have opened a door to expose some of who I am to you, to let you know that you're not alone. To let you see that we all have a story to tell. I have been inspired by so many wonderful women and men who live life on their own terms, who write their own stories. Women strong enough in Spirit to withstand and overcome many storms—women who could stand alone if they had to, yet soft enough to tap into their needs as women to be who they are, expecting to receive love and give love.

I believe in my spirit that this will help someone through to find the courage to step out of her dark place and move into the light of GOD'S wonderful world and see the beauty in herself that she forgot or never knew she had.

*Girl Power Because of GOD'S Power! S.T.A.R.T*

*Come on Girl, it is time to List it AGAIN. Ready to take it to the next level?*

The first step was given to you on the previous pages, if you haven't done it yet. Take some time out to do it. Write on a piece of paper, type in your smart phone, or use the page provided to you to:

- List your Perfections/strengths, and
- List your Improvements/weakness.

The next list I made was a little bit more in depth and more long-term. For this, I suggest you get a Journal/Notebook, or type in your smart phone—whatever is easier to utilize. This should be a dated list.

It's a timeline that would and allow you to see your progress in these areas as you go along. It is said we have 10 major relationships though there are a few others in our lives that we want to have abundance in, or we seek balance in. I know it sounds and feels like a lot, but when you really think about it, when they are all working together in harmonious flow, life takes on a more valuable and potent purpose that gives us our power. We are complex beings; our needs and desires change as we grow.

I didn't make this relationship list up out of thin air. I got this from different sources of learning and surmised what that frame work would look like. I'm sharing what I learned:

- Life and Happiness
- Spirituality
- Bad Habits or Influences
- Fear
- Family / Friendships
- Love
- Career Paths
- Self Confidence
- Money and Abundance
- Health and overall Well-Being

This one includes everything you can think of that would make your life into what you want it to be. The first list was meant to sort of be a written mirror, if you will, of how you see you. The key is to be able to see yourself clearly throughout this journey to finding your Power. It's good to know your weakness, but it is better to know your strengths. Sometimes we don't see them, which is why I suggest you write them out. Doing so allows you not only to see, but to purge, all the thoughts floating in your head. It will assist in giving you the clarity you need, also giving you a reality check when you are seeing it written down. It will also show your growth in the coming days of your evolution into your power. It is of the utmost importance that your list of wants and needs in each category is believable for you. Meaning even if at the moment you don't see how it is going happen, that it is something you could truly visualize having in your life. Dream big, ladies! Dream Big! I know, I am.

I am sharing with you some of what I wrote on my I real list. So, I'm not just talking the talk here. I am walking this journey still. I have a whole lot more than what you see here, so don't limit yourself to three points each. Go the extreme limit of what you want in your life, and no one can judge your courage to dare to dream.

### Health and Overall Well being
- I want to develop a firm body and maintain and healthy weight between 140- 150lbs.
- I want to pray and meditate more.
- I want monthly spa days.

### Money and Abundance
- I want to have at least $100,000 savings in the bank in the next 4 years.
- I want to pay off my mortgage and renovate my home.
- I want to travel more.

### Self Confidence
- I want to feel sexy and desirable.
- I want to be super-confident in my intelligence.
- I want to affirm that I have much to offer.

### Career Paths
- I want to operate my own medical consulting firm.
- I want to help other women find self-love.
- I want to be a business mogul.

### Love
- I want to marry the love of my life and have full partnership mentally, physically and financially.

- I want open, honest, safe and loving communication, and to be his comfort and he my protection.
- I want lots of fun and laughter.

## Family/ Friendships

- I want to build a better relationship with my son and respect his decisions as a man.
- I want to bond more with my nieces and nephews.
- I want to enjoy more moments with family and friends.

## Fears

- I want to step away from my comfort zone.
- I want to be able to speak my mind.
- I want to be bold and unapologetic.

## Bad Habits

- I want to stop over-thinking.
- I want to stop procrastinating.
- I want to stop second-guessing myself.

## Spirituality

- I want to understand GOD'S word and grow closer.
- I want to be open to the infinite wonders and intelligence of the universe.
- I want to live in a spirit of peace and harmony with unwavering faith.

## Life and Happiness

- I want all things, people, places, and circumstances to be in alignment with my life goal.
- I want to know that I didn't give up.
- I want to believe that it is all possible and see it happen.

This one may take some time to put together, and there is no "rush," although the sooner you S.T.A.R.T., the sooner you can make change.

I hope you take the time to write this list. This can be as large or a small as you want it to be. The only limits will be the ones you place on yourself. Open yourself to want to see yourself and what you really want. See yourself—your raw, naked and beautiful self. For some of you, it may give you a moment of revelation that confirms you are already on course for what you want in the various areas, or you could be like me—one who had some re-working to do to get the things I wanted for my life. It is going to be different for everyone.

In going over my first list, I was surprised and really not surprised at the same time. The truth be told, I had a lot more negatives than positives about myself, and I thought my life-list was just a dream of impossibilities. I mean who, did I think I was I fooling? I'm the one who had the thoughts. I saw how unloved I felt. What I realized was that it wasn't lack of love from others, but lack of self-love for me. How could I know how much I wasn't in love with myself?

I never took into consideration that I felt I was unlovable to others because deep down I was unlovable to myself. I was sad, angry and deflated. I couldn't understand why I felt the way I did. For a long time, I struggled. For a very long time, I lacked the vision and the wisdom to turn my pain into power. I was truly living in weakness. I felt no one cared or believed in who I was.

On the surface, I was this woman who looked as if I had it all together and didn't need anyone or anything. I wasn't quite sure how I was sending that message because I was anything but. I just did what I had to do to get through. I wasn't one to depend on anyone for anything. I was scared early on and learned the lesson that I couldn't depend on anyone but myself. This was learned the hard way. There were many lonely nights of tears, fears, confusion and feeling lost, as my whole life was unraveling like a cheap knit sweater. Being stronger than you are is a lot more work than being dependent upon others for your happiness. Discovering this made me tired of acting stronger than I was because it really got me nowhere; yet, I pressed on because your girl just couldn't afford to fall apart.

The Bible says we are promised an abundant life in **John 10:10**, also in **Jeremiah 29:11.** This means we can have it all, if we seek and trust in GOD. I didn't always believe I could have it all. I put limits on myself and my GOD. Once we clear out the clutter of our minds, we can then begin to not only see, but also receive and achieve clear focus—and a bit of old-fashioned expectation. We planted the seed when we wrote out our life plan, now it is time to water, feed, speak life over it and watch it grow strong.

# Chapter Five: And then... S.T.A.R.T.

I n my lowest moment, wading through the muck of

my mind, I was in a state of despair. I needed desperately for something good to happen. I needed a miracle, to hear the voice of God. I wanted to know what to do. I couldn't hear anything. I went back to revisit the lists I had written to see if I was missing something, still nothing changed. I cried what seem endless tears and I prayed like I never had before, still nothing. I was about to give up and, then it happened. One fine day, it came, and I heard a message. It wasn't God's actual voice; it was however the one I believe was used to communicate what I had been seeking was here. I was invited to join a woman's restoration life reset conference call. The call was facilitated Intuitive life Coach, Shannon Evette. This two-hour call put it all in perspective. It was the catalyst that began to change my life, though not right away. I heard a word that clicked, and the voice said, "**S**top **T**alking **A**nd **R**oll **T**enaciously," in other words *"S.T.A.R.T!"*

I have come to believe God places people and circumstances in our midst to lead us to act on what we are meant to do. We don't always hear or see because we are viewing and listening in the natural. God talks to us and shows us in the Spirit. When we miss out, it is because we are operating of our own will not God's will. I continue to labor with discernment. My God-walk has been one of challenge and change. I am learning to connect with God on my level. We are born to win and are given everything we need to do so.

We must take the journey to know our gifts. Fortunately, some of us find out earlier than others, and that is great. All things happen in due season. I believe this is my time... my season of ultimate breakthroughs and elevation in all the areas in my life. If you are reading this, know this is your time now, too.

Back to word on high, S.T.A.R.T., As I was on the call, I listened to the message intently. Normally conference calls don't hold my attention but this one did. I was immersed like a body of water. I heard the message; it touched my spirit, and I was totally amped up. I wanted to soak up every bit of what was being said on the conference call. I tried to write down every bullet point, word for word, I still have those notes. I wrote as much as I could and made big mention of highlights, as they resonated with me. I didn't want to miss or forget a thing. I just knew this was the answer to what I needed. At this point my soul was so desperate for a breakthrough; I was game to try almost anything. Shannon Evette's inspiring words captivated me for as long as the call lasted. Then I hung up and went back to my real life. However, the wheels were turning in my mind and all at once I had a rush of thoughts, ideas, questions, after soaking in all that I had learned. It all sounded so darn simple and awesome. Now balloon has been blown up... *But...* S.TA.R.T. where? S.TA.R.T. what? S.TA.R.T. how? Oops! Pop goes the balloon. I was lost. Suddenly, I felt defeated again, and yet there was something in me that knew I had to keep moving forward. I was killing my soul softly. I was just tired of being tired. I was sick of being sick. I was determined to fight through that feeling of self-deprivation and despair. I knew this current state of being was not supposed "to be" my meant to be. I knew there was more to this life. I was called to something awesome and beautiful.

The life I dreamed of wasn't my current reality—and, not even close. I was determined to break those chains that held me captive. I was determined to seek a life worthy of my living. I felt I deserved a much more fruitful life. I was going to silence the voices that said I could not have it all or that I was not good enough or deserving. I kept asking myself why can't I have it when God said I was born to have an abundant life? HE didn't mean abundance in only one or two areas of my life; HE meant ALL areas in my life. HE means ALL for your lives, too. It was a promise. It is our birthright. It is mine, yours and ours. So, let's go claim it and live our abundant life, ladies.

When you know who you are and whose you are, there is nothing on this earth that can add to or take away from your rise to greatness. I had to learn the hard way. I looked to others to validate me and was disappointed every time. The power was all in me, just like Captain Planet said. I know I am aging myself but so what. I'm good with my graduated life levels. I had to see me. I had to fall in love with my beauty, my gifts, my heart and my calling. I don't have the secret formula for the love-self potion tucked away. This power is readily available to us all if we seek it out. There are still times when self-doubt and dislike creeps up to rear their ugly head. There are happenings that attempt to push me away from the strides I have made to be comfortable in my own skin unapologetically. I accept that I have them, and I seek to find peace and repaint the picture to one of beauty again and smile. No longer do I allow it to take a rest in my spirit and keep me low. I chuck it up to being human, and I don't let it fester and grow like weeds in the midnight hour. I don't linger where the enemy plants and hides its vices of destruction to tangle me up again. I go through it, and then I get moving on to the journey of my joy and of my confidence. I haven't mastered my life; I don't have it all figured out; nor, do I have a crystal ball to see into my future. I just have vision enough to know I can absolutely shape my future to be what I want it to be. I just know that it is going to be great.

Back in the real world, everyone is seeking the one meaning in life that will make it all worth it. I think the meaning of life is different for everyone. I don't think we are limited to one meaning. I think we are multifaceted, multitalented and beings of unlimited potential. We are all on a quest to live a purposeful life, whatever that is. I don't have the answer to what the meaning of life is for you; that is something you must discover for yourself. My meaning in this life may be different from yours. We are not created equal in our gifts, our call or our purpose, though we are all born with intrinsic characteristics. We are custom-made in our own kind of wonderful way. We are not mass-produced products. We are made with care and are priceless. We are one of a kind creation, we are originals. We are God's masterpiece, and we come fully-loaded with everything we need to thrive.

There is a calling for my life that is bigger than I have imagined. I would love to change the world with words of love and empowerment; however, first I had to love and empower myself. Everything we do and everything we are begins with believing in God's greatest creation, ourselves.

> *"Everything we do and everything we are begins with believing in GOD's greatest creation, ourselves."*
>
> *~Tawayna Nicole*

I know now I have given too much power over to the negatives in my life. By allowing those negative thoughts to fester, I simply let more and more in. I know that if I want respect from others, I must first respect myself. I know if I want love from others, I must first love myself.

46

What I know is that I am a woman learning to stand in my own power. I know that I am deserving of a phenomenal life. What I know is the only one who can hold me back from what I desire in the world is me because God made me a promise that said I could have the desires of my heart, if I seek him. As women and, more importantly, human beings we are in control of our lives and how it progresses. It's a mindset. Every great person of note will tell you it is in part the power of your mind that will govern your walk in this life.

I don't know for sure that one can have complete mastery over who they are because I'm not there yet to say yes. I'm still evolving. I believe that our mind, full thoughts and emotions must be in alignment with the plans of the universal movement of God. I think we have a great deal of control over our lives as it pertains to its outcomes. God gives us free will to choose the pathway we take. I believe God has true mastery over us because HE knows what we will do before we even do it. Whereas, we are constantly learning new things and growing, or at least we should be growing and learning. We surprise ourselves sometimes at what we can accomplish. Once a person thinks they know everything there is to know, there is no longer a desire to seek and learn to evolve. We get complacent, stunted and go nowhere slow. When we cease to learn, we cease to expand and grow. When we cease to learn, we have no purpose to meet in life. And, what is life without purpose? For a long time, I did not know my true purpose. I had no direction. I was merely existing and not living.

No one could have told me I would be writing a book, sharing with you and the world part of my life. No one could have told me I could find part of my healing in putting forth the effort to inspire another woman to look and see the beauty inside herself she never knew or inspire the one like me who forgot she was beautiful and deserving. My wow moment in all of this is the list I shared with you earlier. One of the things I had written in October of 2015 was that one of my desires was to help someone with my story. I had forgotten some of what I wrote, and to my surprise I was reminded. Well, low and behold, I am doing it. I am sharing my story. I'm in my S.T.A.R.T. mode. Roll with me ladies; just roll with me.

# PART III

*Little Miss not so perfect...*

I tried hard to be "perfect." All I wanted to do was just get it right, whatever I did. I was everything to everybody, yet I was nothing to me. I sure was "perfect" alright—a perfect mess. When you overcompensate, you don't always recognize that is exactly what you are doing. I was always doing too much and not doing enough, if that makes any sense. I did things trying to overcome what my mind decided were my shortcomings. Sometimes I even said to myself, "Girl, you're doing way too much." I guess subconsciously my insecurities just wouldn't allow me to stop doing, like I had no control at all over them. There was no red light to make me pause on go, go, go. I was full throttle to nowhere fast. Sometimes I still go above and beyond, which really is ok to do at times. Certain situations may merit the call to duty of extra love or attention. When I extend now it's with definite discernment, peace and control. I can combat the tug between my heart versus my mind when it's trying to say you must show yourself approved.

What is interesting about all of this, is that if you didn't know me and met me, you would never know I have any insecurities for the most part, or at least as far as I could tell. I have often found the loudest and most obnoxious one in the room to be the most insecure and I made it my business to tow the line to be a cool as possible. Not exactly sure who cool was but it worked for me. I always chose to keep my personal struggles to myself. I never saw the point of exposing what nobody really cared to know or help with anyway. I would guard my true thoughts like Fort Knox. Nobody wants to be around a person who is constantly feeling inadequate and needy even if they love you. It is draining. It is way too much work to make a person feel secure in who they are when they really don't believe you anyway. There came a time when I couldn't always control my insecurities; they controlled me, and it cost me a hefty price. Little did I know it was the price I had to pay to find me.

## CHAPTER SIX: The sting of Validation

Too many women look for validation of our

womanhood, our essence as a woman and/or our beauty through the lens of a man. In some cases, we seek it in other women as well. I can hear some of you saying while you're reading this, "Oh no, not me. I don't need my validation from a man or anybody else." Well, I'm here to tell you you're lying. Yes, I said it; yes, you are lying. We have all sought approval from others at some point or another. How else do we know what the parameters are in our greatness. How do we know if we are doing well? We have various focus groups in our lives, though you may not see it that way.

I tend to think having various life focus groups somewhat governs what our next big thing in life should be, or how we should look, walk, talk, act, etc. It is evidenced by what and who we surround ourselves with. We want to be where we are celebrated, not tolerated. We want to be remembered, and we want to be loved. We want to be great and to leave a legacy. I believe All these things are forms of approval. The truth is there is nothing wrong with being acknowledged or approved. The problem comes when we let what others think of us totally dictate and define who we are. When we lose complete selective power of our being, it becomes a complicated and problematic issue. If we let what others say and do make or break us, it is not good. Remember we all, men and women alike, are born with our own special individual gifts, and they may not always meet the approval of others. It is great if someone thinks you're awesome, so long as you already know how awesome you are!

We live in the age of the attention-seeker. We are the generation of I. Meaning, *I* must be seen; *I* must stand out; *I* must be relevant somehow, by any means necessary. How that attention comes, good or bad, doesn't seem to matter to some, so long as it is attention, then life is good. It's likened to a drug addiction. It can lead to destructive behaviors. It's even more-so evident in the availability of social media, which dictates what is acceptable and what is sexy, what's not etc. Women but black women, are inundated with esteem- crushing images, daily. For every empowerment message there are two that degrade in some fashion. Who we are and what we are should not be dictated by family, friends or outside influences such as the fashion industry and society to say what makes us beautiful. Black women have always had a more challenging struggle added to us than other women. For a long time, the so-called mainstream industry standards did not even apply to us. We were never considered a true symbol of beauty. There were not many representations of black beauty out there for impressionable young girls like me to see. Even in our own communities, we had warped images of what a beautiful black woman is. We were defined by our skin color, size and shape. It is bad enough when the world defines your level of worth; it's worse when the rejection comes from within.

The color lines and fineness of features was that a darker-skinned woman was maybe not as beautiful as a lighter-skinned woman regardless of her features. I saw it and, to some degree, experienced the comparisons growing up. One of the lines I got from some as it pertained to my looks growing up was, "You are really pretty for a dark-skinned girl." I never knew how I was supposed to respond. It never felt like a compliment to me. It got to be where I hated hearing it. It was giving me a complex, making me question my appeal. It truly is offensive and disrespectful, in my opinion. When I was younger, I wasn't sure why people said that. I am completely aware that such commentary is a result of ignorance. It's like saying for a black person you're smart. If someone says such a thing, you are immediately offended and ready to fight, as you should be, because your intelligence has nothing to do with color, and neither should your beauty. The ignorance carried over in my adult life when I encountered men who uttered those words. I would often hear it as a young girl growing up; however, the difference between then and now I quickly correct and let them know how insulting they are being. The looks on the faces are priceless and ones of confusion especially when I ask if I was, supposed to be ugly because I'm dark-skinned. Beauty doesn't have to be qualified for any reason other than your eyes see it. In that secret place there was scar that formed as a result of such comments over time.

Part of my journey was to discover and find the root of the low self-esteem beginnings. I struggled a bit because some of my earlier memories were faded, or I may have blocked them out for reasons I don't know. If I had to use my biggest guess, it would be that the planting of that seed would have been done during the natural growth process where my own eyes began to awaken to my own body and began to pay more attention to how others saw me.

My uncertainty with my beauty was based on what I saw that considered to be the standard of beauty. As a little girl growing up, there was not much representation of me anywhere. The elementary school I went to didn't

have a large population of black children. I went through a stage in my life where I did not want to be black. It didn't matter that Mommy and Daddy told me I was beautiful just the way I was. I saw color, and mine wasn't the "right" shade. I remember putting a towel over my head and pretending to be white with long silky hair. I was an eccentric child to begin with, I liked things most of my peers didn't. Being black was not beautiful to me at the time. I didn't know I was lost. I thought life would be better just by being of a different hue. I had the attitude. I mean it was easy to fit into that environment and not where I lived. It was my levels of exposure, it had the greater influence.  Mommy would just let me be who I needed to be, though she would lovingly remind me that I was not white and never would be.  I was black, and the towel would not miraculously turn into Caucasian hair. It just seemed better to be anything other than me. It took me well into high school before I embraced my skin. That was only the first of self-esteem issues to come my way.
...

Somehow, subconsciously, I took on the burden of requiring the concern and approval of others whether directly or indirectly. My body matured early, so I was a boy and man magnet before I fully understood what my growth changes would bring to me, or even as it related to my interest in the opposite sex. It made for very uncomfortable encounters.  I did not know how to handle such attention at a young age. I was not at a level of maturity where I could effectively be in control of my sexual development. My mother did her best to explain the changes in my body, and we talked about sex. We talked about the beauty and the pitfalls, but I wasn't ready to take it all in. I wasn't a shy kid; I was uncomfortable.  I was sensitive about certain subjects, and I just didn't want to be a part of that conversation.  At that time talking about sex was just, gross to me. Sex was the absolute last thing on my mind.

 As I grew into my womanly form, I would receive many sexual advances with commentary on my physical appearance. After a while it became normal to hear comments about how big my butt and breasts were, and I didn't know enough to think it disrespectful. I didn't like how uncomfortable it made me feel, and yet I felt powerless to do anything about it.

Something happened as tween I never told to anyone not even my mother. I'm not sure of my exact age because I blocked it; all I can say for sure was that it was a long time ago. I think maybe I was around 11 or 12 years old when I was inappropriately touched by a boy I knew. He was an older boy (not sure how old, but maybe 14 or 15) ... anyway, it doesn't matter. What happened in a matter of minutes seemed like hours. In that short moment in time, I don't ever recall being as frightened as I was at that time. His hands, I liken to the mythological creature "The Hydra"—where you cut one head and two more grew in its place were his hands to my body. Fortunately, I wasn't visually bruised, and there were no physical scars to show on me, the mental ones were planted. He was someone I trusted because I knew him. I did not think he would do anything that would hurt me or make me sacred of him. I saw no need to think otherwise at that time or be cautious of him prior to that event. We all went to each other's houses before, so I did not see that as out of the ordinary. It wasn't until I got inside, and he locked the door behind me that I felt uncomfortable, at which point he wasted no time pinning me against the door, touching me in an uncomfortable and unsolicited way. I was asking him to stop, trying to fight him off, and the more I fought the stronger he got. I remember screaming at first, but not hearing myself scream. It was like he had super strength. I managed to break free, or he gave up though I'm not sure which is more accurate. From that day on, I never looked at him with the same eyes. I feared him for a long time after. To him, I'm sure it was not a big deal; to me, it changed something inside of me. I ran into him as an adult, and he was excited to see me. I was resistant. I still felt discomfort in his presence, and I'm sure he had long since forgotten about that day, but I never have although I have forgiven him.

I blamed myself because if I had not gone to his apartment, then he would not have tried to do the things he did. With time I thought I had put what happened away and moved on. Little did I realize that was another tiny message seed planted in my brain, waiting to be watered to grow like weeds—the messages planted of not being loveable and a worthless toy. Amazing how a tiny seed like that grows to have such a powerful impact. It was one that I had not even considered as part of my self-esteem issues until now.

*The hurt young girls grow into insecure women.*

# CHAPTER 7: Hurt Girl / Insecure Woman

It is awkward enough growing up a girl without any added outside messages, subliminal or overt. Little girls today are even more sexualized than I was when I was one. The changes in our bodies, our emotions, finding out who we are and what we want to be when we grow up are all tremendous pressures.

Your earliest validations come from the love of your parents and other family members. Some of us are blessed to have loads and loads of it in the first important years of our lives. It is very important to have those messages of validation when you are young because it helps to formulate a sense of self. So many young girls (and boys, too) get the wrong messages extremely early in the form of an abusive parent or other traumatic experiences.

You never quite know the full impact of things that happened until you have time to reflect. My parents separated when I was six years old, and I saw through the years how that affected my mother. Little did I realize that time was creating the formula for my future relationships. My father was present, just not as active. I wished he would have been, but as I understand it now, that is hard to do when you don't live with them. As a parent you do the best you can as the non-custodial parent, under the circumstances; still, it's not the same impact as if he lived with us daily.

I saw how my father would spend a night here and there, and then leave. Adults do what adults do, and I as the child growing up saw it as normal because I didn't know any better, and it was just my life. He was a acting like "full-time dad," a family man on some weekends, family trips holidays, and a part- time dad the rest of the time. I didn't know it was numbing me against relationship happiness. There were no expectations; it just was when it was, and when it wasn't... well, it just wasn't. I was living in the innocence of a child. What did I know of my mother's pain? I was cool every time Daddy was around. Then, the worst thing that could happen to a parent did. My father died in what I felt was a most critical part of my life. I was a teenager—a time where I needed the most guidance from a male perspective. He died without even saying goodbye, or that he loved me. For a long time, I internalized that feeling. It wasn't a topic of discussion. I kept that feeling close to my chest. I guess it would be fair to say I had "Daddy issues" that unfortunately could never be resolved because he wasn't here to set the record right.

I think this has affected all my relationships in some way. I wouldn't get too close in subconscious fear of abandonment, or I would cling on too tight for the same reason and be let down. There were very few I even got close to. I have pretty much been a loner by my whole life. It really was just the flow of my life. My dysfunctional normal.

We are now adding to the self-esteem list the subliminal messages through television, movies and magazines that told us what beauty was and, even more so now with the inundated messages spewed via social media, has such an influence in our lives. As an adult woman who is supposed to know better, I too fell into becoming a victim to social media feeds that showcased nearly naked women with damn-near perfect bodies, even the made by surgery ones. Over the years and through several relationships, I have gained and lost weight, never quite being disciplined enough to maintain the size I felt most comfortable at. When you get honest you do see the root why. Truth is the fluctuation of my weight itself wasn't my issue, it was that self-worth demon ever lingering and ever present that has held me in a bondage of discomfort. The goal right now is no matter what my weight or size dress says, is to recognize and honor I'm that chick who is phenomenal.

The internet is filled with sexualized images. I am always one to acknowledge another woman's beauty. I could somehow easily see in others what I failed to see in myself. A beautiful woman is a beautiful woman and the beauty I speak of is more than just the physical. I didn't see my own true beauty; I couldn't see nor embrace my own feminine power to feel I was desirable or intoxicating in a way that drew people into my physical and spiritual space, where they didn't want to leave.

I don't know at what point I began to secretly envy youth and physical attributes. I don't know how I got there; all I know is I was making myself crazy and sinking into depression. I was struggling with several things but the obvious, being time moving away with my age recognizing that I was not as young as I used to be. My face was showing maturity that I had not yet mastered. Mortality was flashing across my eyes. Suddenly the clock started ticking faster and faster and I had nothing of worth accomplished in my mind. My physical frame was undesirable to me. I was not in love with my love handles, or my pooch. It was just a bunch of shit floating in my mind that compressed upon my tainted view of who I was. All I knew was I would rather be anything, but me yet again.

The delirium of depression had me feeling very inadequate and quite unattractive. It pushed me far back to a moment in time where I was weak and felt complete shame in what I had become including my body which was the outward representation of the inner being. This is the seed planted that added to my self-esteem issues. I was around 19 years old my son was almost two years old and I had put on a few pounds within in the 1st year after he was born. Prior to his birth I had been rather slim. Initially after having my child I went right back down to the size I was. Then it happened, I went from wearing a size 6 to a 12. In those days wearing anything close to double digits in clothing was considered "fat" and to some degree it still is. I see it now it is being womanlier but back then that was like death to my attractiveness. I promise you I didn't even notice how big I had gotten. Life is happening to me, I was a young mother trying to finish school, and get a job to take care of my son. I sure wasn't thinking about how I looked. When I look back now, I really wasn't all that big, considering the weight I gained in the latter years ballooning up to where I was almost in a size 24 clothing-wise. I don't know the weight. I didn't believe in scales I believed in how clothes fit. I still don't believe in scales all they do is depress you. I only really get on one when I go to the doctor though I have one at home (No battery in it) just for looks.

Here is where the subconscious mind injected more negativity. I was still young, when I got into relationship with a guy who was not my son's father. Deep down I knew going out with him would be a poor choice, yet I did it anyway. That intuition is real I advise you to listen to it. In this case I did not. So, I said what the heck, at first things were going better than I had anticipated. The whole relationship took me by surprise. In the beginning he treated me well. He was very generous with his money. He would always pick up things for my son and had no problem doing things with me and for me without me having to ask. I even got an allowance, how about that. I did not know all of that came with a very high price. I knew him from my HS days, and I remember not liking him at all. I thought he was spoiled, arrogant and just a jerk. He felt like he could have anything and anyone he wanted. When he would approach me, I always brushed off his advances. A couple of years later I saw him at a gathering, and he seemed like he grew up, matured some from those days. Because of that he was finally wear me down enough to be in his presence. Still a bit leery but I decided to give it a whirl and date him. It must have been me being a mom that softened me because he weaseled his way in at a venerable time. In hindsight I think it had to do with lack of self-worth that I didn't know I had. Quickly the relationship became mentally abusive, and I didn't' see it at first. He would always make snide remarks here and there about my weight. In the beginning I would ignore him because this was the me, he chose when our relationship began. I felt that if it were a problem, he would never have been with me in the first place. So, my defense and clap back would be me telling him I'm not the one taking off of work or parking the work truck, [he worked for the telephone company at the time when people actually had real landlines and phone booths on the street], in front of my house during business hours to be with me so it must not be too bad; after all he was still with me. The truth is after a while it gets to you, the constant reminders of the obvious. I know I gained the weight and it low key bothered me. I started to internalize the ridicule; though outwardly rebellious, deep down I was hurt and very much affected by his words.


There were many other things during that relationship that only until recently, I called it what it truly was. He was abusive emotionally towards me, and he even violated me sexually. How do you tell when you believe it was your fault and you deserved it? I stayed in that relationship longer than I should have. I believed him when he said no one else would want me because of my weight. That was such a low point in my life. All I can say is thank God the Almighty gave me the strength to leave that toxicity forever. I forgave him in the spirit to free myself from that bondage. I saw him some years later, and he apologized for how he treated me and attempted to connect again. I laughed at him in his face and said never and walked away. Life looked like it was rough on him. All I will say is that karma is very real. Over it.

God and the universe have a way to take care of those who willfully hurt one of HIS. I hope he prayed for forgiveness. I had to make peace with him in my heart. I had to stop wanting to see him bleeding on the street, so I could just step over him. God got me over those thoughts because it was not my nature to be so cruel, and it stopped me from healing. He wasn't worth my soul. I know now it was not about me, but a deficiency within him. It took a while to undo the damage caused by being in that relationship with him and here, I was now, a full-grown woman no longer in my twenties, about to undo all I worked hard to get over by feeling less than.

Let's fast forward to a more current time. I am going through a midlife crisis late 30's early 40's. I'm still in my 40's by the way, just the later ones. I was driving myself crazy; thinking and feeling I'm never going to be able to compete with the new concept of what beauty and sexy is at my age. I was not comfortable I my own skin. I am getting older yet not quite old feeling out of place. I was not growing in grace. It was more like feeling as if I was disgrace. We know aging is a part of life, and if you live long enough, you will change physically. While there are now technologies to alter your looks, your age they have yet to change. So, anyway, here I am with my imperfect body in my ever-present fight of battling weight, getting older and not happy with the direction my life was going. I was spinning out of control.

There was a point during my weight fluctuation where I didn't feel sexually appealing or desired, at least not in my head. These feelings, in part, took a toll on my self-esteem, which filtered into my relationship with a man who meant a great deal to me though we are no longer together. I didn't know how to communicate to him just how uncomfortable I was. I took it upon myself, without even having a dialogue with him, to assume I wasn't as attractive as I should be. I looked at the work he did which I thought I could handle. His work had him around lots of women most of whom where young and beautiful. I tried to believe that it didn't matter because he still made his way home to me. I didn't set my emotional and spiritual standards, I placed no boundaries, and all of this is really surrounding around low self-worth issues ones I didn't think I had until exposed when you break it down; none of which was his doing. He has a great presence, high energy, magnetic personality and everybody thought he was a pretty stand up dude, at least that was my observation. He was like a superhero to me, he was smart, well read, he made me laugh, challenged the way I thought about things, he felt safe, there was no fear or worry when he was around, it was when he wasn't with me, I felt unsafe. We had some great moments and some not so great. No relationship is always up. When it worked it did and when it wasn't, it didn't. I think we were a lot a like in a few ways which didn't serve us well. We were in and out of relationship with each other, for a very long time. I allowed it to happen and ultimately, I made it easy for him to overlook things. My inability to communicate what I was feeling didn't help either. Some nights(He worked the overnight shift) if he wasn't at work, I worried while he wasn't with me, he was with some other woman who was "better than me". My insecurities went from zero to 100 sometimes. I kept quiet about it though. I never shared those feelings. The secret shame in me. I blamed myself when things weren't going well.

My first negative thought was always my weight and then would create a list of other possible inadequacies, not pretty enough, not adventurous enough, not cool enough, not spicy enough, not smart enough, not tidy enough, just plain ole not enough. I could go on and on. It was insane and I held it ALL in. I did things that only an insecure woman would do. I did what I never thought I would. I went looking for trouble and I found it. I know relationships take two willing partners; he had his issues we all do. His story is not mine to tell. He just happens to be a part of mine. What I had going on didn't start with him, it's just what was added that helped manifest in an undesired way. I can take responsibility for my part.

In all honesty, there was not one time I can recall in our relationship where he said anything negative to me, about me or made mention my weight being problematic for him, or that it would jeopardize our relationship in any way. He never shamed me for my body. I had a fixation that just because he didn't say it, doesn't' mean he has not thought it. Like I said we are a like in a few ways.

There were other things and other challenges, some my creation and some not. Part of it for me was surrounding my looks not being sexually desirable or not providing mental stimulation that give life to spark "she's the one". It just created a plethora of problems in my actions. And somehow, I felt unworthy, and it translated in other actions. My secret shame now revealed. What you think about, you bring about—and boy did I bring it.

I can say now that I was the one who had the real issue. I never verbalized how I felt because for one, I did not know how, did not want to deal with the confrontation and I knew it was the ravings of a crazy woman. Yet, I talked myself into believing I just wasn't good enough. So subconsciously I felt I had to prove my worth which was disastrous. I was having flashbacks to a relationship where my weight did matter, and in that relationship, he did say mean things, and did things to hurt me. He made sure I knew I wasn't perfect quite often. I went to the highest levels of security threats, Code red. My insecurities were on high alert. I was brainwashed. The seed of negativity had a hold on me. It was deep rooted like ragweed's that don't die they just grow differently.

I had been going to therapy for years to sort out some things in my life that had nothing to do with what I have just shared. These occurrences with my mate took place well into my therapy journey. In the natural course of therapy my current relationship discussions would take place. Therapy was one of the best decisions I ever made. Though it was not a 100% cure to my issues, in many ways it helped me put some things into perspective and gave answers to some of the "why me" questions. I recommend seeing a mental health professional if you are suffering in your mind and spirit. Prayer helps, but it also helps to talk to someone who can guide you through. Just like you see a doctor for your physical ailments, you should take just as much care of your mental health because it does, in some part, affect your overall physical being.

My therapist would encourage me to talk over my issues and concerns with my mate, and I would flat out tell her I couldn't. I gave the excuse I didn't think he would listen or take me seriously. She gave her professional opinion on my response, and she would still advise me. I would tell her I would find the courage to and I never did. It was all fear- based. There were also other things I withheld for the same reason. The **F**alse **E**vidence **A**ppearing **R**eal (aka FEAR) was taking over my life. I was afraid of the truth because I was not ready to act. I took it upon myself as I do most things, to think his thoughts and speak for him. I quietly began to consume more and more discomfort for the sake of my fake comfort. Somewhere along the line, I lost my sense of self-worth. Now that I think about it, maybe I never really had it to begin with. I was like a runaway train about to jump the track and crash, and that is exactly what I did when I collided with myself, and I was already in therapy at this time. Thank God I had my therapist for the support because she forced me get honest and work it through.

I tried too hard to be a "perfect" person. It did not work because I had to realize I'm not perfect; I'm human and fallible. How is it I accept imperfection from others and not myself? How do you see the beauty in others and not see it in you? I was doing too much, yet not enough. Not enough for myself. This super woman having-it-all-together stuff is exhausting. I was running on empty cylinders with no gas and was nowhere near a filling station for my spirit. It was all bound to stop. I finally admitted it was ok to not have it all together, and those who love me will do so no matter what. Though I still struggle with that some, it freed me and it's not as prevalent in my life as it once was.

I am NOT every woman as Chaka and Whitney had me singing, declaring, and almost believing. I can't do everything "naturally." I have to work at some things. While I am a "super" woman," I am not Superwoman. Guess what, I am ok with that. I don't want to be every woman or Superwoman anyway. I just want to be the best Tawayna Nicole possible. I laugh at myself because I really am just an awkward black girl in a world, with a colorful past and vibrant future, full of love joy, fear, dysfunction, pain, gifts, order and hope. I would rather laugh than cry.
My ministry of being a woman who is all things to all people has been too tiresome with little to no reward and guess what? It still wasn't enough.

I can't be the voice for all women, as we are each unique in some way. Sure, we all have the same anatomical features we were born with that make us female; however, even with that we vary in shape, size and genetic makeup. Our theme music is different, though I do think we share a common core in desire. We all want some degree of admiration; we all want to be our most beautiful selves and to be respected as human beings and—whether it be internal or external beauty—we want to be appreciated for who we are and what we do. I also think, most importantly, we all want to feel and be loved. What is most important is to love yourself more.

Ladies, there is absolutely nothing wrong with letting a man who loves you expound on what you should already know, which is how beautiful you are. I'm going to raise both hands for a quick second after I type this to cosign. I love hearing the man I love say how much he appreciates me as much as any woman would. It feels and tastes better than my favorite wine. It is even better when it comes from a spirit of genuine love. The potential problem with this comes because they can tell you a million times and show you in a million ways that you are beautiful and that they love you, and it won't be worth a damn unless you see your own beauty and love yourself first. I'm not just talking about the outer shell; I am talking about the inner beauty—your mind, your heart, your spirit and the gifts you have to share. You must tap into your own beauty... learn to love who you are. Know what you represent, and don't be afraid.

We must begin by healing the little girl inside us. Tell her all the things you wished somebody would've told you. Write her a love letter to heal her and free her to just be. It then allows you to be that captivating woman that God meant for you to be.

## CHAPTER 9: Where I'm from/ Where I'm at; But God

What I didn't know then was that God was

going to transform my pain into purpose. I didn't know everything I experienced in my life, from the time I reached the age of accountability until now, were the steps to get me right here at this moment. HE had to let me walk this road, whether I chose consciously or unconsciously. HE knew it would ultimately lead me to not only seek HIM, but trust in HIM completely.

Reflecting on that time, now I see I had angels watching over me every step, though I sometimes felt very alone. God was always there; I just didn't allow for His full presence. Here I go with another song lyric, this one by the Clark Sisters. "It would have been me/it could have been me/it should have been me if/it wasn't for the blood..." I tell you there is a song for almost every area of my life... But God.

"When you are down to nothing, God is up to something. He may not come when you want Him, but He's always on time." I'm sure we have all heard those sayings hundreds of times. I will admit they were just sayings to me with no real meaning. I acknowledge and understand that they are more than words to me now; they are valid in their message to the believer. No matter where you are and what it looks like from your perspective, God is real and is working to take care of your needs. When I look back over my life, so far, I remember some of my actions that were not well thought-out. God was protecting me from harm; He was blessing me with protection and forgiveness. Ladies, I could have been dead, yet Jesus kept me... Just like the song says. I am so thankful for to Him for saving me and for showing up on time. "I started from the bottom, now I am here," in my Drake voice.

By all accounts, I had a comfortable life growing up; though it was not without challenges. We weren't rich, but I never lacked anything. My mother and grandmother made sure we had what we needed and wanted. I am sure my dad did his part; I just couldn't really see what he did the way I could see Mommy and Grandma. There was never a lack for love or affection in my formative years. I was just, in a word, "different." I did not really bond with the people around me. Not sure why exactly, and part of me was ok with that.

Like I said earlier, my father was always in my life. He and my mom were separated when I was six years old. I didn't get to have him long because he died before I turned 16.  I had a strong family support system. I had people who loved me growing up, yet I still struggled with connection. I was very much a loner growing up, and I didn't have a lot of friends. The good thing was I didn't have much conflict either. I pretty much kept to myself. When I did have conflicts, I don't recall entertaining any. Truth be told, I was oblivious, and I could not have cared any less, nor did I want to know half the time the people who didn't like me.

My family and a few close friends were very protective of me. They handled my issues that I didn't even know were issues.  Like I said I did not care.  I wasn't a scary person. I just couldn't be bothered with things that weren't important for me. I have a talent for being in a room in body and not in the room in mind, if you understand what I am saying. I felt like if you didn't like me, so what? My life didn't stop because of that. It really was a defense shield because, deep down, I would care, and it would hurt; you just wouldn't know it. I wasn't a troublemaker or fighter. It was like I lived in a bubble. I guess my nonchalant attitude about things gave way to some of the misconceptions about who I was. It still happens today. Now I am more aware and sensitive to it. I try to look for constructive ways to correct the misunderstanding of my personality. As I grew older, I began to fully understand—from observation of countless others—the fewer friends you had, the less conflict you got into. So, I don't have any regret in that because the few friends I did have were genuine and are still in my life today.

Now to explain why I didn't connect to my own family was another story. I always felt different, out of step and out of place in my own family. I wasn't very social, as my sisters were. I wasn't very close with any of my cousins, but there was nothing but love. We always had fun when together. I found my comfort in my maternal grandmother; it was with her I felt my most relaxed and ok to be me with my eccentricities. Grandma just let me "be." I could wear a house coat (it was like a robe and made like a dress) that she made for me to wear around the house. I would put on my good shoes, wear her good jewelry and let my imagination soar whether it was dancing or playing teacher with my blackboard and fake students. She was truly my "no judgment" zone. She allowed me space and opportunity for flow of spirit. She demanded much of me in that she wanted to see me do wonderful things. I never felt inadequate if I did wrong around her—not that I got in trouble with her for anything I did. I was perfect in her eyes. I spent a lot of my time in self-inflicted isolation and, quite honestly, was content with it. I didn't think to know any better. I saw nothing wrong with it until later.

Most people would assume by my facial expressions and my quiet demeanor that I was mean or snobby. Quite the contrary, the truth was I was neither. Forging friendships was not so easy for me. Part of me felt inadequate in some way. I would always be the quietest one out the group. The truth is I am not all that quiet if you catch me in the right setting. When people thought I was bored, I was having fun. I enjoyed being around lively people; I wasn't the extrovert though with the right tribe I'm extra fun. I think I genuinely confuse people. There are many sides to who I am as a person. I just don't have names for them, and they are all me. Everyone does not get the same connection if any at all. This came, I guess, as a result of how I could not connect to people in my own family growing up.

I don't make friends in two seconds of meeting a person, that's all, and if by some miraculous act it happened, that meant we were soul connected. I do not consider every person I know my "friend." I have many acquaintances, very few friends. The ones I call friends are deeply loved.

I can't reveal who I am to everyone as they might not be accepting, or they are not persons who mean well in my life. Some would call it hiding, maybe even being false. The one thing I can say with all certainty is that I'm not a phony. Either I liked you, or I didn't. And because I liked you didn't mean you "knew me." You knew what you needed to know for the time and place. I never hid who I was. Whatever I gave of myself to people was genuine. I just wasn't going to allow just anyone and everyone into my private world. If I let you in, believe me, you were super special.

Though I have grown in many ways to be more inclusive and social, some things have remained the same. I still have few tried and true friends who see the mess that I am and still manage to love me. I don't know how they deal with me sometimes. I am super thankful that they do. I have evolved in that I have not completely closed the door to receive new friendships either. The change came about with the evolution of my self-confidence along my journey in accepting who I am and not worrying about who does or does not like me. I like me better, now. I am free of whatever kept me from being so open. Won't God do it?

Who I am today versus who I was yesterday battling with who I "thought" I was versus who I "really" am has changed considerably.

My adult years have been slightly different. I was on a mission to be as perfect as I could be. I was set to be Wonder Woman and Super Woman all in one. So, ask me how that worked out for me? I can tell you in a word it was a disaster. I was a woman who had it all together, but not quite as together as it should have been.

To the outside world, I was a teenage mother who overcame the odds against a girl who has a child before maturity and no active participating father. It looked like I was making a come-up. I didn't drop out of high school; I went to college, even though I did not complete my degrees'. In my ignorance and short sightedness, I ended up trading college for an immediate marketable skill. I went to a business school instead because I didn't want to have a single mother living on welfare tell me how you did it story to paraphrase Tupac. My mind was not set up for "the struggle" not realizing to focus on college was the thing that would prevent that very thing from happening. I needed to work and provide for my child and I did that. In hindsight, I should have just finished college first. I don't "regret" my choice though. I look at it now as it was just my journey. I have been able to become rather successful in my career choice. I continue to enhance my knowledge-base as it pertains to my career path.

I thought it was a badge of honor to say that I didn't use men to support me financially. I didn't rely on a man to "take care of me". No damsel in distress here. I was an independent, working, single woman who put her child through private school. I was able to care for my son, and he never went hungry or worried for much. I didn't shirk from my responsibility as a parent, and I owned my mistakes or so I thought. Overall, I was doing well. Sure, I could have done better and been better off financially if I had made better decisions along the way. Analyzing this from different lens, I also see how this way could have translated the wrong message to a man in that he was not needed in my life because I did it all myself. Of course, that was false I needed more than I could tell, and I always thought a man would be an enhancer to my life not the creator of it. God had the creation part already handled. Hindsight always gives you that perspective. I beat myself up constantly for what I thought I lacked, or what I didn't do.

In all that I did accomplish, I forgot to celebrate. There was not enough self-praise. I only focused on what I didn't do and what I could do better. I didn't celebrate that I was smart, had a kind heart, and that I was an overall a great person. I feel it's time to write a love letter to myself and ladies you should, too. Self-love is super-important. It gives you power; it gives you strength; and, it encourages you, but most importantly it validates you in a way that no one else can.

I was a woman quietly struggling with her identity in terms of understanding "who am I to be in this life, and what my purpose is." A woman with massive insecurities, a woman who took her gifts for granted, minimized her deeds, depreciated her own worth... and just like that... I just wasn't good enough. That stinking thinking got me jacked up in the head.

Have you ever found yourself at a crossroads with no idea on how you got there? Have you ever wondered how your life has gone down the path it has? Then, say what now? I think we have all at one point—no matter our station in life— wondered about that.

Whether we have achieved our dreams or put them on hold, there is always the "what's next," "what do I do now," and/or "was it worth it" type of self-assessments. In the song sung by Diana Ross, the questions asked are:

- Do you know where you're going to?

- Do you like the things that life is showing you?

- Do you get what you're hoping for?

- When you look behind you there's no open doors. What are you hoping for?

- Do you know?

So, I ask... do you know? I have asked myself that question a million times over among other questions and was never quite able to answer because, in truth, I didn't know where I was going. I didn't know what I was hoping for, and there always seemed to be closed doors. I cheated myself and didn't even realize it. I wasn't asking myself the right questions to get to the truth. Asking the right questions will always lead you to your truth, for better or for worse. So, the question was this:

What is lacking in me that holds me from achieving abundance, success, love and complete joy in my life?

Then, the answer was this:

Nothing but yourself because you are fully equipped with everything you need to achieve all you want in this life.

The follow up question went something like this:

If I have all I need, then why am I not elevating in my life the way I should be?

The final answer was this:

You lack belief, and you are allowing fear to hold you back. You don't feel you deserve to be elevated. When it registered that is was my lack of belief being part of the reason, I simply couldn't "believe" that was the answer and rejected it. How about that? I would not believe that I didn't really believe. I thought it a preposterous idea. I believe in myself, I thought, and sure I deserve better. Why wouldn't I?

As I began to move out of the denial stage, I finally got honest, admitting there are many areas of my life that were plagued with doubt. I was operating silent to the world out of fear, one that was crippling and detrimental to my growth. The voice that was once a whisper grew loudly, instilling in my spirit that I am not good enough. A voice so deafening I couldn't hear the call to greatness. I didn't trust it was real; I didn't think I was ever meant for anything that remotely spelled out what the Bible said in that I would be complete, whole and lacking no good thing.

# CHAPTER 10: Until

I n my greatest despair, I conjured up every fear and

insecurity I ever had, and they appeared boldly before me. Good Lord, it was frightening to see how many there were. They were like a loud mob ready to beat me down into subjection. As the noises got closer and louder, I began to scream. I was trying to find my voice again. I was afraid it was going to overtake me and drag me into darkness forever. I yelled loudly above the voices of my doubts and fears because I had to get them quiet. I had to silence them forever to rid me of the pain and to hear God's call to my greater path.

I heard the song *Breathe into Me* by Fred Hammond, and it was a like window to my soul. One of the lyrics is "Commendation tried to hold me like a prisoner in chains." That was how I felt, like a prisoner suffocating. I couldn't breathe and was being held hostage to myself. I was dying a spiritual death and needed new life. I just didn't believe it was fair that I suffer the way I was. I know I was meant for more than the hand I had been given to play out as my life. On my knees in prayer, endless tears, I began to speak death and slowly began to kill the voices of not enough so I could see the masterpiece in me.

What I could not see at the time is that God dispatched His unseen angels in the form of my sisterhood to cover me when I was weak. These ladies are some truly awesome women who have prayed with me and for me. They have let me cry and never once passed judgment or parceled out unsolicited or unwelcomed advice. They always listened and stayed neutral when I just needed to vent. They held me with love. They know who they are, and I am grateful they were near to help me find my footing and rise to the occasion.

I allowed myself to process each different emotion or thought I ever had. In my soul revision, I discovered that God was always there protecting me and covering me. I was secured from my first foolish decision to my newest one. Discovering that I wasn't being punished or being left alone, after all was an eye-opener. Little did I know that God was just waiting on me to tap into Him to reveal my power in and through Him.

"Girl Power Because of God's Power"

*Jesus said in Mathew 19:26, "With man this is impossible, but WITH GOD ALL things ARE Possible."*

When you hear the call that will move your life in a new direction, that is not the time to ignore. It's easy to miss the call because of so many false voices speaking into your life. I can testify; I'm the Queen of missed the calls. When you've made so many mistakes, it's hard to trust your next move is the right move.

Here is the thing, for us to grow and know what works and what doesn't, we just have to do. We constantly ask ourselves the wrong questions, like "what if it doesn't work," whether it questions a relationship, a job, or an idea for something like writing a book, for example. I have a better question to ask, "What if it does work?" Come on now, Woman...

Just S.T.A.R.T. "Girl Power Because Of God's Power"

If He gave you the message, it is yours. It's your lesson to be learned and tested. You already have the passing grade; it's up to you to keep it. It's not something you have study for; God gives you an open book test. Seek out the answers. So, let's GO!

*Girl Power Because of Gods Power...*

In every woman lives a little girl who has felt powerless, and no matter what station of life we are—rich or poor, high school dropout or a PHD—we've been sent back to that place of vulnerability in public or in secret where we feel loss of control in our situations. When you feel like giving up, DON'T!

You are where you need to be. Embrace where you are, and see why you feel the way you feel, then use it to come out of that feeling. Where and who you are today is not where and who you were yesterday. Use it to make another move forward and use it as fuel to add to your untapped power to thrust you into a place of elevation.

*Girl Power Because of God's Power...*

Every tear you've cried waters your garden of beauty to bloom. Every trial and every challenge is used as fertilizer in your soil, and all you have to do is plant the mustard seed of faith to grow it. Your promise is grown from your pain.

**_Remember, you are all these things and more:_**

- You are a worthy.

- You are a blessed woman.

- You are God's woman.

- You choose to be happy.

- You intend what you want for your life.

- You trust in He that created thee.

In taking care of others and trying to please everyone else, my soul's resources were depleted. It was time to take back and claim what is my birthright. It was time to take care of me. I was ready to be whole, secure and proud of the woman I am called to be. I want to do and be what I am called to all in love and in the service of GOD.

### Finding my call: "Let's get happy"

I didn't know what my purpose was and wasn't sure of my gifts.
It challenged me. I was stuck in the "less than" way of thinking so long, that to conceive that I could reach for more was almost unthinkable. When you live a life filled with incompletions, half stories, almost had its—which we all know that song by Brandy that says "Almost doesn't count"—you start to doubt what it is exactly you were put on this earth to do.

I never once thought I would be of any great service on this earth, but that was my old way of thinking. I allowed the imagery of what others thought, and my own fears, to hold my life hostage and in bondage to the "it's never going to happen for me" thoughts, and the "this is my lot in life, so just accept this as such" syndrome. I just wanted to be "happy" and *that* was my "BIG Goal."

Sounds like a huge and almost impossible dream if you in any form thought the way I used to. Then, the question becomes what is "happy." What would define it? I am what they call an over thinker, and I tell you I can tear apart a thought. I will analyze my own analytic conclusions. I think you get my point.

I never really thought much on happiness, or what it took to be happy. That was just a God given gift in my early opinion. The irrefutable logic was that you were born happy, you grow up and, in my case, would meet then marry "Prince Charming" and live happily ever after... just like in the fairytales and made for TV movies. As the realities of life have shown, life is not in the ways of a fairytale, though there is some underlining truth in them because quiet as its kept there was struggle before the happily ever after.

So... ok... let's ponder that for a second. Back to this let's be happy thing. First define "happy." What exactly does that mean, and how do you propose to be happy in a state of doubt and discord?

The Dictionary's definition of happy says it is a "feeling or showing pleasure or contentment, cheery, merry, joyful jovial, jolly, jocular, gleeful, carefree, untroubled, delighted, smiling, beaming grinning, in good spirits, in a good mood, light hearted, pleased contented, content, satisfied, gratified, buoyant, radiant, sunny, blithe, joyous, beatific, more fortunate and convenient. Synonym: fortunate, lucky, favorable, advantageous, opportune.

In looking at the definition, it doesn't say anything about how you become happy, who is able to be happy, where you get happy, why you are happy, or length of time this "happy" state is. It just says these are indicators of being happy. Then decided to find out but, I asked some questions first.

- How do I get it?
- Can I buy it?
- Is there an automatic happy button I can push and suddenly it happens, or do I have to work at being happy?
- Do I depend on someone else to define my happiness?

I thought if I had more than enough money, I would be happy, when that didn't happen instantaneously, I was like so, now what? I thought if I had the admiration and love of my mate, and were married, then I would be happy. Well, that hasn't happened yet. I went down the list of what ifs. If I bought new shoes, clothes, bags and dresses jewelry etc. I thought for sure if I lost weight, I would be happy. It was none of those things mentioned. I don't think I was satisfied with anything.

My relationships (pretty much all of them) suffered. I was in the mist of this battle in my head and the struggle to find my happy place. There was a point when nothing was doing it. I was walking in misery and depression.

Have you ever heard that your happiness depends on you? There are many that say you're not happy because you choose to be unhappy. Blah, blah and blah. I don't believe that people consciously choose to be unhappy. I can't imagine a person waking up saying, today is the day I will be unhappy. It makes no sense to me. The human mind is a complex one. I don't judge another's walk. I have been in that space where nothing was soothing my spirit. There were so many people, things or circumstances out of my control that caused my unhappiness, or at least I thought they did. My outer surroundings controlled every thought and emotion I underwent. I thank God for giving me the spirit that I have. It quietly carried me until my mind could reframe things surrounding my life to understand what was meant by "choosing happiness".

I felt that I had no one or place to call home, where I could rest my spirit with ease. I felt discomfort and inadequacies everywhere. I couldn't see my purpose. I had no true desire to push for anything. I simply accepted what life threw my way no matter how fruitful or unfruitful it may have been. I fixed what I could and let the rest languish until I could take care of it, or until I forgot it even existed. This must be my life, right? GOD wouldn't let me suffer like this unless I was supposed to, right? Things happen for a reason, right? {Insert buzzer sound here.} *WRONG!* Instead of making my life happen, I was letting life happen to me and taking me into a dark place. I had an epiphany; the true reason I wasn't happy was because of me, myself and I. The wise one's words rang true I was responsible at the end of it all.

I'm quoting Glenda, the Good Witch from The *Wiz because it resonated with me like never before. She said* "The qualities you saw in your friends that they carried all along, that's true for you also. Home is not a place where you eat or sleep, its *knowing...* knowing your mind, knowing your heart, and knowing your courage. And when we find ourselves, we're always home" Those powerful words spoke life to me. I have seen that movie a few hundred times over the course of my life and when I got what she was saying it was a Wow moment and no matter when I see that scene always evokes emotion in me.

If you live long enough, there will be some opposition and push back. There are days when you won't feel powerful. The thing to remember is you are not so powerless. I still have moments that test my strength and sanity. As it would be now, even as I share my journey with you, I face opposition in my life. There will always be challenges to face, and I am not a exempt just because

I have found the light. I have my crosses to bear. I'm just trying to live this life as best as I can.

I am trusting and believing that I will overcome and be victorious. Sometimes the roads we are on in our current lives are because, somewhere down the line, we decided to consciously or unconsciously travel in that direction based on our level of thought and being at that time.

If you are enjoying the sites on the road you are traveling, then keep going until you have reached your destination. If you are like me and may have gotten lost in the woods, desperately trying to get on the road of beauty and freedom to find your way home, you might want to change. Get your battle ax and start chopping one tree at a time until you can see your way clear in the wilderness. Seek GOD in prayer, or whatever higher being you believe in, and you will be directed the rest of the way.

I am not qualified to, tell you who, how or why you should believe in what I do. It has taken me some time to trust in God. I thought I was alone and abandoned by God. I did not always really believe He would make a way for me. I learned if you take one step forward, GOD will make 10 for you. This is the higher being of existence I believe in and call upon. In the Word it says, "He will make roads in the wilderness." (Isaiah 48) I am trusting in the Word.

I know I will overcome whatever challenges me and stand victorious covered in grace to live abundant. "Tears may endure for a night, but joy comes in the morning." In the midnight hour, I will train to awaken to pray for God to shake the foundation of the prison that holds me hostage; to bust open the gates and loose me from the chains. I pray that I may walk free to live do effectual work and prosper giving all the Glory to God for it all. I am expecting and believing my works and efforts shall not be in vain. We have the power to change the roads we travel if we so choose and are committed to doing so.

I am just sharing a bit of my journey with you in hopes that it will let one or all of you know we are not alone in this world, so don't believe you are. I want to make a difference in this life I live. I want the life I live to have some real meaning, purpose and power. The day I close my eyes on this earth, which won't be for at the least 55 years from now, I want to know that I left it all on floor, that I gave it all I've got, that I have touched the lives of those I love and made a positive impact on the world. That I had purpose and there was power in my pain, knowing that without doubt all I had to do was just S.T.A.R.T. finding my girl power in God's power.

When your soul cries out in pain, God hears your cry. I have learned and continue to learn that sometimes we must go through our challenges to allow God to show us that we must trust in HIM

We are in full control to receive all powers in the universe granted by our Source. It all begins in our thoughts, feelings and actions. If we come half-spirited, then we cheat ourselves from receiving the abundance in life that belongs to us. I don't know about you, but I for one am officially tired of being cheated. I am over it! I refuse to be cheated out of my inheritance of infinite abundance. My mind belongs to me, not the spirits of darkness. I was born to receive the light to blossom, so I shall now be open to receive and grow in who I am called to be as a woman. Ladies, all is not lost. You can find you and grow into unimaginable beauty. All you have to do is S.T.A.R.T.

# CHAPTER 11: Let's begin at the end

Where do we begin? All great Leaders, coaches, and motivational speakers say start with the end in mind. They all say to think about what we want to leave this world with that will acknowledge we were here. What legacy would be passed on to our families to carry on for us? In truth, I never thought about the end and hardly ever considered I had a future to plan out. Why think about the end when I won't know what goes on post my earthly existence? It made no sense, I would be dead, and I wouldn't know. Then I considered the possibility of us truly being spirits in physical form. I would live on. I think it would be beautiful to leave something on this earth that could outlive my physical life in a positive way for many generations to come.

I was always one to live in the moment. Why bother to make plans because my plans never worked out anyway. As thoughtful as I was, in some cases I kind of went with the flow no matter how ridiculous it may have been to do so. I was alive and not living; I was existing. Up until the reframing of my thinking came, I had made no lasting contribution to the world I lived in. Truthfully, I really wasn't all that bothered by it for a long time. I really don't know why I felt such feelings. I don't know when it hit me exactly; I began to feel uncomfortable with my life. It felt empty, like there was more that I was supposed to do. It was in lost in the wilderness, then got stuck in a ditch that I fell into, slowly filling with dirt to suffocate me. Like in a bad dream I couldn't climb out. I had no inkling that what I had to offer would even be accepted. Part of me always felt rejected in some way. My mindset was terrible. I needed a shift.

To model those who have been successful in making a difference in this life, I began to ponder those thoughts of how I see the end of my life. For a while, I still didn't know what my end might be. Then it came to me. I know that I want to have lived a life where I left it all on the table and all over the floor with no room to see regret like an episode of hoarders. I want to grow as old as GOD will allow me. I pray I live to see the triple digits with my full wits about me, still full of exuberance for life until I live on earth no more. I know I want my grandchildren, great grandchildren and beyond to never know lack in any form. I want generational curses of mind shackles to be broken. I want to leave a legacy of love and a lifetime of joy that would be passed down to future generations of my lineage. I want to leave a mark on the world that will affect change for the better, one woman at a time. I want my name to live on in the world as a woman who started on a journey in hopes of finding her own path, daring to inspire others in their quest to meet this life on their own terms.

I want my obituary to read more than the origin of my birth, academics, who I left behind and that I lived a long life. I want it to read in part , I was one awesome woman blessed by GOD. I want it to read that I was a woman who lost her fears and stepped out on faith to make a change to elevate her life. I want it to read that I loved my husband and my family unconditionally, and that I shared with the world my gifts and a little bit of myself unapologetically helping other women find themselves. I want it to say I lived an abundant life in all aspects and was a blessing to others. I want it to read I discovered the true meaning of adventure and that I loved God, and most of all I lived life and not let it continue to live me doing it all in love. Yeah, that is kind of what I want it to say. I have learned to dream big, so I can live big and my final call will receive standing ovations of joyous sounds in that I had Girl Power because of God's Power.

I can see myself at an old age remembering the part of my life when I awoke to fight for a better life and sharing stories of parts of my life that taught my biggest lessons. Some stories will be funny and some not so funny, yet all are of me and made me become the woman I am. I do hope my mouth will have a filter because you know old people will say anything and not care. You can't tell everybody everything. I laugh to myself because I remember some things my grandmother should have kept to herself, and she would say to such, "Age has its privileges." I am looking forward to that privilege. I apologize now while I still care to all the burning ears. Bring water to douse the flames.

With finding how I want my life to look in the end, I now have to create that story, which brings me here today for my better tomorrow. Writing this book has been therapeutic for me. I have started and stopped, not sure if I should continue to write. Yet I get called to continue, as if there was really a message I was meant to convey. The more I type, the more I realize I am setting out to prove something to myself. That I didn't give up, that I stayed the course, and that I have taken in all the lessons I have learned and made it a successful life of which I can be proud. I am a winner already, and if you are reading these words, know you are a winner too.

God sets us up to win, so it is up to us to work and show ourselves approved not by man, but by *GOD*. We have infinite power within us. We are resilient beings. How else do we face great hardships and still find at least one moment to smile or laugh about something that took our pain away if only for a second? How else do we get up each morning to face the day not knowing if we will overcome a challenge that has bound us? In the words of Pastor Sarah Morgan, "There is a blessing in the pressing."

I have done a lot of fasting and praying during this journey, and with each endeavor to do so I feel like I only want to push harder, even though there are such trying moments where the enemy is whispering in my ear to just give up and give in. Just like the song by Mary Mary says, *"I just can't' give up now. I've come too far from where I started from. Nobody told me the road would be easy, and I don't believe He's brought me this far to leave me."* So, I can't give in no matter how long or hard it is to wait on GOD for what I am asking for. I must find a way to keep pushing, no matter how many blockades I go up against. With each crossover is the next step of manifestation because it is my birthright. I am entitled to receive my abundant inheritance.

I must be open to see and hear what God is revealing to me. My faith walk is hard... I tell you the truth. The Bible says that if we only have faith as small as a mustard seed, then we can say to that mountain move and it shall be so (Luke 17:6). I found out quickly that my faith must have been smaller than that because no mountains in my life were moving, and it didn't even look like I could move the dust. I had not considered I was blind. To my eye, I couldn't see that I was moving obstacles out of my way. A person who had it all together might not see much victory in it but I was making progress. There was power in my body that moved me when I couldn't.

Each day I wake up and make it through things that try to break my spirit. I move a stone.

During my process of recovery these were my victories. If I got out of bed when everything in me said stay there and got dressed to face the day, I moved a stone out of my way and around that mountain when:

- Each day I was able to find laughter through my tears, even if it was at my own expense.

- Each day when I prayed to God for strength.

- Each day I fast and cry unto God in thanksgiving for another chance to make my enemies mad and weaker.

- Each day, even when my bank account is low, I still feel grateful to have a need met

- Each day that I grow more fearless.

- Each day I have forgiveness in my heart.

It might not have been the mountain of my desires, but it is what I recognize to be God giving me the power to clear the pathway get to under the mountain to shake and weaken its foundation, so I will be able to move it right on out my way with ease. When you sleep walk through life as I did, you miss and waste much time either feeling sorry for yourself or beating yourself up. It's all a journey, a process by which you have had to go through in order to get you to where you are now. Neither you nor I got where we were or are overnight. I didn't go to sleep one night and wake up unfulfilled. There were a series in the chain of events that brought me to that state in life. I am striving to break those chains forever.

When I finally woke from my slumber to see my way clear, I brow beat myself with the "if only" I did this or that, then I would be. (fill in the blank). All that did was sink me further into that ditch I talked about earlier. What I am learning to do is forgive myself and all the errors I have made in my life. Who knows, maybe they weren't errors after all; maybe they were the steps I was supposed to make in order to have a story to tell and share with you.

Every misstep is still a step. Though it may delay you for a bit, it also may be one you had to take in order to learn and continue your path to finding your calling. It might have been to humble you or show your true strength. Just don't stop; keep stepping until you get where you want to go.

Writing this book doesn't mean I am there, and have it all figured out. It just means I grew strong enough to climb out of that ditch to S.T.A.R.T. walking. Along the way I have encountered some missteps. Honestly, I am still having a few. I vow not to give up, no matter what. Even through my tears and sometimes great pain, I won't give up. I refuse to quit fighting and to grow stronger in God and myself each day. I will continue to move more stones until I can move that damn-blasted mountain out of my way and reap the full bounty of my abundant inheritance.

There will be people who will discourage your journey, not so much purposefully. Sometimes, people think they are helping. They don't mean to bring you down. It is a view from a different lens. It may be all they know from their limited perspective. When you know you are purposed to do great things, you must be able to lay it all on the line and risk it all, possibly enduring hardship to get there. God promises us He will give us the desires of our heart. We have to seek, ask and knock all in faith to find, receive and have it open to us (Mathew 7:7).

I am beginning to revel in my Girl Power because of GOD's power. What was set up to break me into shattered pieces, leaving me unable to restore, has failed. I know that it was the spirits of the enemy unseen wanting to dim my light by using my relationships, my finances, and my view of myself with false images appearing real. It' all designed to throw me off and make me give up on any desires I have. I will stand victorious every day I wake up and make a move to a better me and a better life. I am unstoppable. I am unapologetic. I am becoming a woman with vision. This is my time for manifestation. This book alone is my testimony of acceleration.

Seeing my end set the tone for my beginning. This is where I get to re-write my own story, change my history and create the life I want to leave behind. When I am done, I expect to have nothing left unsaid and nothing left undone.

# CHAPTER 12: So, Let it be Written

My test will be my testimony, the first of many I am prophesying over my life. I am here today to tell you I believe in myself a little bit more than I did yesterday. I don't continually fifth guess my actions anymore. One of these awesome days, I will get down to completely trusting my decisions.

I grow more fearless in the choices I make. I decide what it is and live my life unapologetically. I don't overtly seek approval, though I do seek guidance on some things. It is good to have trusted people around you in your life, a personal board of directors if you will. People whom you can seek council as needed to sometimes give you a check and balance in areas you feel you could use assistance. You don't need or want people who dominate your life; you need judgment free people with objectivity that won't attempt take over who you are.

I'm learning not to be afraid to fall, as it is merely feedback for the next level. I can admit it's hard to step out on a ledge where you might fall; I just can't keep being afraid. It's just gotten me nowhere fast.

I have learned the key to abundance and power is that it comes from how we think and view the world. To change the way, you think takes discipline. It is an ongoing progression, and at times it has been difficult for me, still I press on. In seeing me as God sees me, while loving me as God loves me, I gain a renewed sense of spirit. My spirit is grateful knowing God will move to make life for me abundant in all facets of life. The power to change who we are, what we do and what we become begins within. Change of self is difficult for some of us because we get stuck in the negative behavior previously learned. Just know what is learned behavior can be unlearned if you are ready and willing to go all in.

When we can surrender to that change, it is so transformative in ways we see with the naked eye and things we feel in the spirit. You will start to look different. You will begin to act, and you will feel differently. These changes may not even be overt, and they don't have to be, nor do you need anyone to confirm what you already know. It just is, and it is so. That is a fact some people will only see you one way; it happens. In the fullness of your due season is when you will show them better than you could ever tell them. True power rules and moves quietly, then BOOM! The impact is felt. "All hail the Queen."

For a long time, I toyed around with starting my own business as a healthcare office operations consultant. I even went as far as writing an outline of the services I would offer and stopped short in follow-through because I had no direction but mostly out of fear of failure, more honestly. I was afraid to fail, not realizing that I might be afraid to win. Being afraid to win seems like a strange concept because everyone loves a winner. So, what is the fear in that? It reminds me of a poem by Marianne Williamson when she starts by saying, *"Our deepest fear is not that we are inadequate; our deepest fear is that we are powerful beyond measure. It is our light, not our darkness, that most frightens us."*

She is saying we are afraid to shine because winning may change the things, people and places around us. It can, at times, result in you to walking away from people you love, possibly leaving them behind or vice versa. I don't think that anyone wants to leave those they love behind. It could leave you feeling isolated and alone. She also makes you understand that you have no right to deny the greatness God has birthed within you. I never wanted to leave the people I love behind. I want everyone to ride that wave with me. Just like Billy Dee Williams said in Mahogany (one of my all-time favorite movies, by the way), "Success is nothing without someone you love to share it with."

I have reconciled for the first time that I just might not be able to take everyone with me because, for one, everyone might not want to come along. Secondly, they may not be meant to be a part of my story the way it is unfolding. There is no room in my life for regret for what I am meant to do. No longer is ok that I hold myself back or be held on to if it keeps me still. It was in these most recent years that the call for me to step out and do something bigger with my life was sounding the alarm. I was going nowhere slow with all the negative messages in my head. When you can go no lower and are already on the ground, there is no place else to go but up.

There was power and purpose in my pain. While going through my transition I decided to get off that floor and plot out the life I wanted. I joined conference calls and bought several books (some I will share with you later about mind restoration and the power of the mind, learning how to channel positive thinking). I also found a virtual life coach and connected with women and men of

GOD for direction. I attended webinars, and live seminars too. You name anything with self-help, I was willing to get into it. I needed to jumpstart my life.

When the clutter of my mind started to clear, I was able to remember that I wanted to be my own boss woman. My mother always said I was too smart to work for anyone, and other people said I had some brains, too. So... why not shoot for the universe and start my own consulting firm? I decided to take it further than just a thought in my head. I wrote out a sound business plan— one I am very proud of. Then, one day I decided to go for it and take another giant step. I filed legal documents to get my limited liability company (LLC) status. It was no longer an Idea in my head it was real. DobMer PM Consultants LLC was born. The name was a merge of my family names. *My dream was for family abundance not just mine.* It is a work in progress. Being a business owner is not easy and in time I will overcome those challenges and it will be successful. Nevertheless, I am proud of myself and got it started. You have no idea how much of a big leap this was for me. I plan to be a major player in this life I live.

If I am starting a Healthcare business, why write a book? This is a lead off, a testament to my development. It is on my journey of carving out a path for myself. Its self-help, its self-inspired to aspire to help other women who might not otherwise see that she can overcome her pain and thrive in whatever way she chooses to claim as her own happiness.

I felt the call to write my story as it unfolds. I felt that if nothing else, I can show the possibility of how little steps can make major changes in how you feel about yourself. Besides, who says you can't do and have it all?

Each day meets with a new mental challenge to overcome. The battle of the mind is real. Somehow, I could've, would've, should've messages always try to creep in and disintegrate all your progress in making your life work. To stay on your journey and not run out of steam, you have got to stay powered up somehow remembering your why. You have got to get in God's word and teach HIM for yourself. He is the true Source of your power. No one can create that special relationship for you. Gaining a healthy mind will strengthen all other areas in your life. Spiritual growth comes from reading the word of God, other words of power, praying and meditation.

I have kept myself going and motivated by putting me first in that I seek higher levels of being. I affirm and fortify myself. I have all kinds of motivational sayings around me. I have even recorded some in my own voice to listen to. I will share a few with you:

- **"I don't do half way, and I am unstoppable." ~Allyson Byrd, The Money Mover**

- **"My life is filled with abundance in so many ways. The more grateful I am, the more reasons I find to be grateful. I am deserving of all the abundance that flows in my life." ~ Unknown Author**

- **"I am in a Divine Breakout for Revelation, Acceleration and Manifestation."**

- **"I might not be good enough for myself sometimes I am always good enough for God**

- **"In my imperfections, God steps in perfectly."**

I get weak sometimes and become overwhelmed because I want it NOW, and I'm scrambling to figure out how make happen what is not ready to happen just yet sometimes causing my frustration. I shut it down sometimes and zone out everything and everybody even if it's only a few hours to collect myself.

When I feel myself slipping that means it is time to get repurposed and remember my why. First, I go to GOD in prayer, then I will periodically take out the list I have created for myself to be reminded that my purpose is greater than my now situation. I have a vision board with pictures and words that call out what I want in my life. You can also create your own vision board if you choose. I gave myself a deadline as to when I wanted to see the manifestation of the things I wrote out. I faithfully read the bible and study with anointed approved men and women of God who teach me of God's promises. The heavenly Father, through Christ Jesus, is my Power source and my Help.

I am here to remind you that we are all purposed for greater things that will last throughout generations. God is not a seasonal God; He is not parceling out crumbs. He sent HIS only son, Christ Jesus, to die for our transgressions so that we would have wholeness, longevity and live an abundant life in all areas. I don't know about you, It's the life I want live. I believe I can have it and absolutely believe I deserve it. I am calling it into existence for us. I am in agreement with you if you want it. . It's our time to now step into the promises of God. It's time to reclaim our birthright of power. It's time to get in alignment with what goodness awaits us. I feel so strongly that we must move now to gain momentum towards what is ours. We must get in preparation to receive it.

**S.T.A.R.T!**

When we learn that God wants us to walk into our permanent place of abundance, we will stop planning simply for a season and elevate our expectancy. These are revelations that are given to me by my spiritual leaders. God is continually sending people into my life who are meant to show me the pathway to HIM. Showing me that I need to trust and rely on HIM. They are to keep reminding me that my power comes from HIM and within. Therefore, as my sister's keeper, I am reminding you of the same.

This is about owning who you are as a woman, whatever that is to you. It's about holding your own, so you can rise to your calling and radiate a beauty and softness not even you can deny yourself. Fall in love with you the way God has, and anyone around you will soon fall in love with you as an extension of the love you have. I believe that. Ladies, we are on this journey together. If you have made it this far in reading, we are connected in spirit, and know that I pray this will touch you in some way to move more deliberately and to reach for what is designed just for you.

My virtual intuitive life coach, Shannon Yvette, embarked upon a Captivating Woman Tour in order to minister to women and help them find their calling and own their femininity. I was fortunate enough to attend the one in New York City, NY where I live. I was super excited and got to meet her up close and personal. Before that I was attending only her virtual classes. Shannon was beautiful all around, as I initially felt she was. She quite honestly is the reason this book is even being written. She challenged me to step out and discover what it is I was meant to do.

At the Captivating Woman Conference, she called us to step into our radiance. She gave us five principles to:

1. Get in touch with and own our femininity in order to flow and shine in our truth that love makes us better.

2. Focus on our gifts.

3. Walk in freedom and live without fear.

4. Have faith to believe in who we are and what we are meant to do.

5. Embrace fortune, for it embraces and favors the bold.

That conference was awesome and an eye-opening experience for me. None of what is happening now in my life was overnight; it was all an accumulation of earlier happenings. Like I said, I'm not there yet and I still have a lot of work to do. However, this is just one step on the journey to what I am called to do. This time, I know I am headed in the right direction

I have so many books of my writings, always afraid to showcase them to anyone. I thought my words weren't eloquent enough... weren't rhythmic like a song lyric or didn't touch on any deep levels of social consciousness like most poets. I don't have a category to put my writings in, other than it was what was on my mind that I needed to purge. I was inspired to write again and decided to step out of the box and share. These are the first things I have written in a long time. Maybe I will share some of my earlier ones, one of these days—another door GOD has opened for me. I am truly blessed.

Girl Power because of GOD'S Power! Just S.T.A.R.T.!!!

Left intentionally blank

# CHAPTER 13: **Wonderful Words**

*The discovery of me... who I am... my life... my thoughts, and action... may change from moment to moment. The core of me is who I want to know. The soul of me is what I want to show. My quest is to understand who I am, and if the others don't, I won't give a damn. The life that springs from my body comes not from the world; it comes from the heavens, the Creator of the universe. The passions of my life I wish to uncover have more to do with being a better me—more than being a better lover—seeking to discover a deeper level of understanding of the things that surround me, while working towards a better- handling them all.*

*Trusting in who I am, the choices I make, having faith in my journey to be better than when I started and not giving up when present is great struggle. Learning how to juggle the ups and downs, learning how to turn an unfavorable situation around, and still nobody sees the tears of a clown.*

*To create a vision for who I want to be, where I want to go and how I see myself changes from moment to moment. You can't plan for what you expect if there have been no expectations in place. A failure to plan is a plan to fail. With no direction or purpose the people perish, and with no dream to reach life is bleak. Sloth and Idle is the playground of the underworld, the darks hurtful spirits. To complete what I start and submit to the sacrifice of seeing it blossom and grow, I seek fulfillment in self, not seeking it in others. I move from the comfort zone unafraid, bold and strong. The discovery of me....*

*Girl Power because of GOD's Power, yet that doesn't mean life is always sweet. There are times when it's sour. If you are not ready, the world will eat your soul and devour you up like a hungry lion who captured his prey. It's not a game; there is not much room to play when you must stay always on your guard. Therefore, you must pray and obey the Word of God who keeps your peace, not a piece because you are already whole. You are stronger than you know. In this cruel, cold world tensions and malice grow. So, where do you go when reserves are low? Who has your back when you fall off track... when the deck is stacked against you? What keeps you from believing that what you bring the universe is a process of achieving all it was meant to do? You must understand the problem isn't the world; the problem is you... Tell me, who is it to blame when the waterworks fall from your eyes like heavy rain... Do you ever wonder why you cry? It's not always because someone said good-bye. It might have been that beautiful lie we tell ourselves daily about how unworthy we are. It's elementary. My dear, you were born to be a star. You are so much more than believe you are...Your spirit commands the universe chapter and verse, remembering to be blessed and not cursed... It's absurd if you heard you don't matter. Girl power because of GOD's power, this is your time. This is the hour in receipt of your true inheritance and your true reward; come claim it and life is restored...*

*We (I) are/am taking a leap of faith, holding our breath and hoping that GOD doesn't close the gate. Was this fate after all? It's been generation after generation that failed to be great. Greatness is still full of gratefulness; and I ask what we are grateful for. A life of mediocrity? A life dictated by society—the one that tells me who I should want to be, who I should want to see and be seen by? So, blinded that I can't see me? This is the struggle, questioning who is she and what is me? Could I really be what dwells deep within? Am I still held hostage to the original sin? Is Jesus truly coming back again? I can't stop the raging inside that says I was born to win. Dissatisfaction trembles my world like a 4.0 earthquake coming into and trying to thrive in a world I didn't make, working around a system that systemically wasn't created for me. Its sets me up to live in poverty—as in where the impoverished mind, soul and spirit live morally bankrupt and corrupt—leaving me to be heartless and thoughtless, yet none of these things am I. Heart I have so, I don't qualify. Thoughts sings like R. Kelly said, "I believe I can fly..." Dorothy and Patty asked if blue birds fly over the rainbow. Why can't I? So, why can't I? After all, everything in GOD's Word said I was born to thrive. Isn't that the reason Jesus died to save my life? So that I can live in the light? I can say mountain be moved. I'm not confused. I just refuse to believe in the darkness. I simply refuse the harnessed shamed for my fame like a harlot when I didn't start this. I finally learned in my life I am the "Artist." I can paint my perfect picture bring to life a vision in my mind... I am not confined. My life is a Masterpiece. God is the Mastermind.*

*There is power in the words "life and death are in the tongue," and we've only just begun to have fun with those wonderful words of aggression and passion, feeling stronger than a whip giving you a good lashing is not bashing... creating a space to think and inspire action... to gain traction. But you don't hear me, though the whispers in the wind... you let them blow. You'd rather stay in the dark than know to grow... in the light. What stifles you more in your life is letting fright eat your words like a parasite...*

Tawayna Nicole/Just START

# Self-Love Letter- Dear Woman

Dear Woman,

I tell you what you mean to me. First and foremost, I love you deeply. I want to tell you just how proud I am of the woman you are becoming. You have stumbled along the way and, at times, I know you were tired, weary; just about ready to give up and give in. You have gone through tremendous trials in your life journey. You've cried more out of pain than of joy. The pureness of your heart never gave up on those you loved, no matter how flawed they were. You sacrificed your happiness at times, so that others would discover their own happiness. You gave so much of yourself to others and not much to yourself. I am here to tell you that YOU ARE AN AWESOME WOMAN!!!!!!

What hurt me deeply was that you could not see your own beauty and your own worth. You devalued who you were. You would too often shrink to let others appear larger, and when their voices got louder yours simply became background noise. I didn't know how to get you to shout, and for a long time I let you languish in your obscurity.

I am sorry for what I allowed to happen your life. What I have come to understand is that you had to go on this journey to find you/me. You had to go through to get to where you are at this very moment in your life. God has always protected you, even in your darkest of times, and HE has loved you beyond your own love. I write this with tears in my eyes because my heart is so full of love for you. It is in overflow. I want to make sure your soul is cared for.

I want you to never doubt that you have made positive impacts on the people who are connected to your life. You absolutely deserve an unconditional love, to be protected, cherished honored. Remember that it all begins and ends with you. You deserve wonderful moments that happen in your life. You are beautiful inside and out. You are a one of a kind Masterpiece. As you elevate on your journey, always stay grounded in God's word for it will be your salvation. There will still be some rocky roads ahead; just stay the course. You have come too far not to keep going. Your life is filled with much to be grateful for in abundance. You have everything you need to achieve what you carve out in your life. Remember who you are and whose you are. I love the woman you are and continue to love you, too. Time is not your enemy it is your guide.

There are no limits in this life except the ones we place on ourselves. We've Got Girl Power because of GOD'S POWER!!!

Let's GET IT.......

# Biblical Scriptures

**Biblical Scriptures I have read for Inspiration:**

*James1:5* - *If any of you lacks wisdom ask God who gives generously to all without finding fault, and it will be given to you.*

*1 Samuel 2:2* - *There is no one holy like the lord; there is no one besides you; there is no Rock like our God.*

*Romans 8:37* - *In all these things we are more than conquers through him that loved us.*

*Colossians 4:5* - *Be wise in the way you act toward outsiders; make the most of every opportunity.*

*Jeremiah* 20:11 - *But the Lord will make me like a mighty warrior, so my persecutor will stumble and fall and not prevail. They will fail and be thoroughly disgraced; their dishonor will never be forgotten.*

*Deuteronomy 8:18* - *But remember the Lord your God, for it is He who gives you the ability to produce wealth, and so confirms His covenant, which He swore to your ancestors, as it is today.*

*Mathew 21:21-22* - *Jesus replied, "Truly I tell you, if you have faith and don't doubt, not only can you do what was done to the fig tree, but also you can say to this mountain, 'Go throw yourself into the sea,' and it will be done. If you believe, you will receive whatever you ask for in prayer.*

**Psalm 27: 13-14** - *I remain confident of this: I will see the goodness of the Lord in the land of the living. Wait for the Lord; be strong and take heart, and wait for the Lord*

**Deuteronomy 20:4** - *For the Lord your God is the one who goes with you to fight for you against your enemies to give you the Victory.*

**Matthew 7:7-8** - *Ask and it will be given to you; seek and you will find; knock and the door will be open to you. For everyone who asks receives; the ones who seek will find; and, to the ones who knock, the door will be opened.*

# Resources

*My Mentors:*

Pastor, Minister, Life Coach, Intuitive Healer

**Follow them on Periscope, Twitter, Instagram and Facebook.**

- **Carla R Cannon** -
  http://carlacannon.com/about-carla/

  Books Written: The Power in Waiting and

  The Entrepreneur Blue Print

- **Minister Naisha Cooper** -
  http://naishacooper.com/

  Gumbo The recipe for Righteousness

- **Pastor Sarah Morgan** -
  http://www.womenofvisionla.org/

- **Shannon Evette** -
  https://www.facebook.com/ShannonYvetteEvolveDaily/

  Books Written: Worthy


 **A few books I have read.**

"Power vs. Force" by David R Hawkins PHD

"Fervent" by Pricilla Shier

"Abundance Now" by Lisa Nichols

"The Power of I am" by Pastor Joel Osteen

Tawayna Nicole/Just START

"Leave your Mark" Allyson Byrd

" Afformations" By Noah St. John

"Think and Grow Rich, a Black Choice,  Napoleon
Hill/Denis Kimbro

Making Life Work........